UNSEALING ANCIENT MYSTERIES

KARI BROWNING

Unsealing Ancient Mysteries
by Kari Browning

Printed in the United States of America

ISBN 9781628715477

Unless otherwise indicated, Bible quotations are taken from New International Version, Copyright ©1973, 1978, 1984, 2011 by Biblica, Inc.; the New King James Version, Copyright 1982, by Thomas Nelson, Inc.; and The Orthodox Jewish Bible fourth edition, OJB. Copyright 2002,2003,2008,2010, 2011 by Artists for Israel International.

www.xulonpress.com

TABLE OF CONTENTS

The Internet can be a great source to answer questions that arise as you read this book. The magic of quick researching by search engines, such as Google, will lead you from one source to another. I encourage you to search the Web, especially where I haven't cited extra-Biblical sources.

There is a Glossary at the end of the book that will define terms that you may not be familiar with. These terms are marked with corresponding numbers throughout the book.

Scripture references throughout this book contain words that have been capitalized and put in bold type for emphasis.

The Hebrew name for the Messiah, "Yeshua,"[1] is used throughout this book, instead of the Greek name, "Jesus," as a reminder that the Messiah was Jewish and was raised in a Hebraic culture.

"If there's a book you really want to read but it hasn't been written yet, then you must write it."

~ Toni Morrison

"It is the glory of God to conceal a matter; to search out a matter is the glory of kings."

~ King Solomon (**Proverbs 25:2**)

Forewords

"What a marvelous work you hold in your hands! It is like a treasure chest of revelation to enrich one's understanding of ancient Scripture.

In the days of what I have come to call "the Coeur d'Alene revival," Kari Browning rose as a prominent leader of the outpouring in which God opened the heavens, pouring out signs, and wonders, and miracles. Although this revival may be lesser known in contemporary moves of God, nevertheless it touched thousands worldwide with refreshing and delight.

It was in the days of this outpouring, I began to minister frequently with Kari in an effort to bring forth the Kingdom of God in its fullness. Having spent hours and days ministering with this great woman of God, I quickly began to notice she had a keen sense of timing regarding people, places, and dates. Effortlessly she could call forth people and places and correlate them to significant moves of God on the earth. I could see her gifting as a ***prophetic chronicler of the times and seasons***.

Prior to many events, the Lord would reveal to her a number, date, or something out of His creative order, to enlighten her regarding the desire of the purpose of God in the event. One of her favorite sayings when this revelation would occur was, *"It's a sign!"*

It is with this unique gifting, the Lord has given her the ability to look both behind and beyond the ink of Scripture and mine out the language of Scripture unknown by many - especially as it relates to the Festivals of the Lord.

Allow Kari to take you through Scripture with the lens of the festivals as a background of past and future events. I assure your delight and encouragement in what you will discover.

Randy DeMain
Kingdom Revelation Ministries

"Embedded in the writings of Moses, we discover extraordinarily significant prophetic implications outlined in the Seven Festivals of Israel.

They are described as God's **divine appointments** with mankind illustrating His complete plan of redemption. To fully appreciate them, we must return to an understanding of the Hebraic culture as it relates to the New Testament application of these truths.

That is precisely what Kari Browning has done in her book **Unsealing Ancient Mysteries.** Kari beautifully captures the meaning and relevance of the festivals as they relate to this generation.

We are living in a time when "Latter Rain" revelation will begin to perfect the Bride of Christ without spot or wrinkle and empower the "Sons of the Kingdom" to do the greater works; a time when profound *secrets* and *mysteries* of God are discovered as hidden manna for the hungry heart; a season when the Spirit of Truth falls upon the Scriptures to give us great revelatory insight.

As Kari teaches in her book, by appreciating and understanding the festivals, we can more strategically posture ourselves for what is coming and ultimately mobilize God's people into the great harvest. To that end, **Unsealing Ancient Mysteries** reads like a manual providing biblical and historical evidence of the importance and application of God's festivals as we prepare to move into this great juncture of human history."

Paul Keith Davis
WhiteDove Ministries

DEDICATION

I lovingly dedicate this book to Harold Eberle. Harold, you and I have disagreed on the subject of the end-times for years and, as a result, you stirred me to write this book.

As you once said, Harold, *"If someone disagrees with you, you probably just haven't explained it well enough!"*

Acknowledgments

Iwant to express my gratitude to those who have helped me in publishing this book, **<u>Unsealing Ancient Mysteries.</u>**

A great big thank you to Joseph Good, who first introduced me to the subject of the Biblical festivals over 20 years ago. When I saw you on TBN, my heart leapt at the truth you were sharing. I've never found anyone who has come close to understanding this subject like you. I will be forever grateful to you for introducing me to this fascinating subject.

Thank you, Mike, my husband of 33 years. You've always encouraged me, supported me, and believed in me. Your help with the household responsibilities during the writing process was very much appreciated. I love you.

Thank you, Mark Golden, for all the time you've spent with me at Barnes & Noble, and the practical suggestions you've given, to make this book a reality. Your editing skills and input have been invaluable. I couldn't have found a better editor.

Thanks to all my students and members of my congregation over the years, who loved the teaching on the festivals and encouraged me to write this book.

I owe a debt of gratitude to all who have prayed for this project to be completed. I'd like to especially thank Amy Bunjter and Bridget Mixon, two of my dear friends, who have been so faithful in prayer.

Thanks, Melissa Williams, who challenged me to set the time aside to write and helped me to come up with a plan! You are an amazing life coach and dear friend.

Thank you, Brandon and Jacquie Walter, for your love and encouragement and being such loyal friends to Mike and I over the years.

Thank you, Joshua Browning, for being so amazingly creative and designing the front cover.

A special thank you to my sister-in-law, Linda Heneghen, who watched endless hours of Joseph Good videos with me when I was desperately trying to understand these concepts so many years ago. Linda, you've also inspired me to write this book and here it is – finally!

This book is the result of 20-plus years of research. I'm indebted to countless authors and teachers whose books I've read and lectures I've listened to. I don't remember all of your names, but thank you for sharing your revelations.

INTRODUCTION

But you, Daniel, keep these words secret, and seal up the book until the time of the end. (Daniel 12:4)

I've been on an exciting journey to understand the Biblical mysteries that have been sealed up until this time in history.

I've found a key to unlock the mysteries and I want to share that key with you!

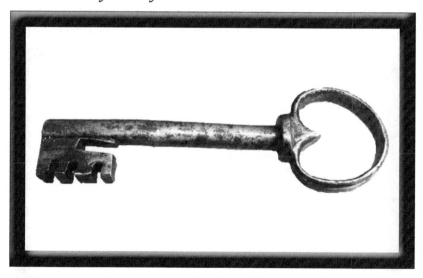

The *key*, I believe, is found in Leviticus 23. When we understand the Biblical festivals outlined in that Bible passage, it opens up revelation about end-time mysteries.

The biblical term **mystery** refers to "a secret from the Lord."

Your God is indeed the God of gods, the Lord of kings and a revealer of secrets. (Daniel 2:47)

There are mysteries that can only be understood by comprehending the Biblical festivals and the language and customs associated with each festival. These festivals were given to the Jewish people by God to teach on Yeshua's First and Second Comings. This concept will be developed in depth throughout this book.

Behold, I tell you a MYSTERY: We shall not all sleep, but we shall all be changed, in a moment, in the twinkling of an eye, at the LAST TRUMP. (1 Corinthians 15:51-52)

Did you know that the *last trump* is a synonym for the festival of *Rosh Hashanah* (Feast of Trumpets), that teaches on what is commonly known as the "rapture"?

Each festival has specific language, names, customs, and liturgy associated with it. When we become familiar with these, certain difficult passages begin to make sense and we start to see the overall plan of God.

My journey into the *mysteries* began a couple of decades ago when I was watching television and a Bible teacher by the name of Joseph Good was teaching on this subject. My heart leapt and I knew this man had discovered an amazing key to understanding the Bible. I eagerly awaited his program every week and devoured his material.

Unfortunately, his teaching felt like *college level* and I was still in *preschool.* I kept plodding through the teachings, even though I didn't understand much of them. It felt like I was being given pieces to a huge jigsaw puzzle. Then one day, after much perseverance, I saw the bigger picture. Now, I want to share this teaching with you, but I'll warn you beforehand that some of it may be very puzzling!

To you it has been given to know the secrets of the Kingdom of God; but the rest are taught in parables, so that they may look but not see, and listen but not understand. (Luke 8:10)

My goal is to make this complex subject as easy to understand as possible. As Albert Einstein once said, *"If you can't explain it simply, you don't understand it well enough."* I like that.

The controversy surrounding end-times, in my opinion, stems from the lack of understanding about the festivals listed in Leviticus 23. I'll explain in this book why I believe the Spring festivals teach on Yeshua's

First Coming and the Fall festivals teach on Yeshua's Second Coming.

So don't let anyone pass judgment on you in connection with eating and drinking, or in regard to a Jewish festival or Rosh-Hodesh² or Shabbat.³ These are a shadow of things that are coming, but the reality is found in Yeshua. (Colossians 2:16-17)

I'm hopeful that this book will challenge you to study and understand end-time theology by understanding the Biblical festivals. We're told in Psalms 89 that we're *blessed* if we understand the symbolism of the festivals.

Blessed (happy, fortunate, to be envied) are the people who know the joyful sound [who understand and appreciate the spiritual blessings SYMBOLIZED BY THE FEASTS]; they walk, O Lord, in the light and favor of your countenance! (Psalms 89:15, Amplified)

Chapter 1

MUCH OF THE BIBLE WAS WRITTEN IN FESTIVAL LANGUAGE

I believe that we need to understand the Hebraic mindset, the Hebraic culture, and the festival language of both Daniel's and Yeshua's day to understand the Bible better.

Then what advantage has the Jew? Much in every way! In the first place, the Jews were entrusted with the very words of God. (Romans 3:1-2)

A good example of the need to understand the customs of the time is illustrated in the following passage.

Else what shall they do that are baptized for the dead? If the dead are not raised at all, why then are they baptized for them? (1 Corinthians 15:29)

If you read this passage about being baptized for the dead in its context, you see that the Apostle Paul, who was a Jewish Rabbi, is teaching on the doctrine of the resurrection of the dead. There was a Jewish custom of ritual washing and immersion in a mikveh[4] of a Jew's dead body prior to their burial — the word *baptize* can be translated "to wash." I believe that the rhetorical question Paul was asking was, *"Why bother washing the dead bodies if there is no resurrection?"* This passage was not advocating that people get baptized in proxy for the dead as some sects have interpreted it to mean.

The Bible was written from a Hebraic mindset. Unfortunately, the Greek way of thinking has strongly influenced our Western culture. Plato was a Greek philosopher. Along with his mentor, Socrates, and his student, Aristotle, they helped to lay the foundations of Western philosophy that has greatly influenced our thinking, even in the Church.

Plato taught Gnosticism, the belief that the material world should be shunned and the spiritual world should be embraced. This is not a Hebraic concept.

Well, whatever you do, whether it's eating or drinking or anything else, do it all so as to bring glory to God. (1 Corinthians 10:31)

When you adopt the mindset that the material world is evil, you cannot truly enjoy life. Yeshua came to give us life to the full. **(John 10:10)** The Jewish people knew how to feast and how to throw a party as we'll see as we explore the festivals listed in **Leviticus 23.**

Listed below are some differences between Hebraic and Greek thinking. See if any of these ways of thinking sound familiar and have influenced the way that you believe.

Hebrew – Relationships are ultimate
Greek – Knowledge is ultimate

Hebrew – Assumes the existence of God
Greek – Existence of God must be proved

Hebrew – Focuses on community
Greek – Focuses on the individual

Hebrew – Believes in the supernatural
Greek – Believes in what can be experienced with the five senses

Hebrew – Reveres and honors age and grey hair
Greek – Worships youth and vigor

Hebrew – There is one God
Greek – There are multiple gods

If only we could take off our Greek glasses and see through Hebraic eyes!

I've been on a wonderful journey to understand the Hebraic way of thinking, the culture, and the language of the festivals. In doing so, mysteries about the end-times are being unsealed.

Chapter 2

THE FESTIVALS TEACH ON THE FIRST AND SECOND COMING OF THE MESSIAH

The festivals listed in Leviticus 23 were given to the Jewish people when they left Egypt and when they arrived at Mount Sinai 50 days later. They were told to celebrate them as a *perpetual* (ongoing) ordinance.

Instructions on how to celebrate the seven festivals in Leviticus 23 were given to Moses when he ascended Mount Sinai for 40 days and received the Torah[5] and the Oral Law.[6]

The Oral Law today is codified in the Mishnah[7] and the Talmud.[8] Orthodox Judaism[9] believes that most of the oral traditions in these books date back to God's revelation to Moses at Sinai. According to Orthodox belief, when God gave Moses the Torah on Mount Sinai, He also gave him all the details found in the Oral Law. Moses subsequently transmitted the Oral Law to his successor, Joshua, and the tribal elders, who passed it on to their successors, in a chain that is still being carried on. (Ethics of the Fathers 1:1)[10]

Some aspects of the festivals were not required during the wilderness wanderings. For example, it was required to wave the firstfruits of the harvest on the Festival of Firstfruits. That particular instruction was not instituted until the Children of Israel reached the Promised Land forty years after leaving Egypt.

In **Deuteronomy 16:16**, God instructed the people to come to Jerusalem three times a year to observe the festivals.

Three times a year all your men must appear before the Lord your God at the place he will choose: at the Festival of Unleavened Bread, the Festival of Weeks (Shavuot/Pentecost) and the Festival of Tabernacles (Sukkot). (Deuteronomy 16:16)

The Jewish people observed festival ceremonies both in the Temple and in their homes. Many of the instructions for these ceremonies are found in the Mishnah (the Oral Law), in the section called Mo'ed that teaches on the festivals. *Mo'ed* means **"appointed time."**

The Jewish people have an **appointment** to be at a specific place (Jerusalem) at a specific time (the three major festivals). Also, God has an **appointment** to perform certain events on festival dates. The festivals are both historical and prophetic.

There were times throughout Old Testament history when most of the Children of Israel would fall away from celebrating the festivals and then a righteous leader (judge, prophet, or king) would restore the practice again. For example, Ezra reinstated the celebration of *Sukkot* (Feast of Tabernacles) after the Babylonian exile.[11] (See Nehemiah 8)

In Leviticus 23:2, it is written that the festivals of the Lord should be holy convocations. The Hebrew term is *mikrah*, which means **"a rehearsal."** God gave the festivals to be yearly "rehearsals" of future events! We need to understand why God instituted the festivals and what He meant to teach through these prophetic rehearsals.

The festivals correspond to the agricultural seasons in Israel. The rains came in two primary agricultural seasons known as the **former rain** and the **latter rain**. Thus, the Spring festivals were associated with the former rain and the Fall festivals were associated with the latter rain.

He will come to us like the rain, like the LATTER and FORMER RAIN to the earth. (Hosea 6:3)

Therefore be patient, brethren, until the coming of the Lord. See how the farmer waits for the precious fruit of the earth, waiting patiently for it until it receives the FORMER and LATTER RAIN. You also be patient. Establish your hearts, for the coming of the Lord is at hand. (James 5:7-8)

In understanding that the Spring festivals correspond to the former rain and the Fall festivals correspond to the latter rain, we can surmise from these verses that the First and Second Comings of Yeshua will correspond to the Spring and Fall festivals.

Chapter 3

IMPORTANT EVENTS HAPPENED ON FESTIVAL DATES IN THE PAST AND WILL HAPPEN ON FESTIVAL DATES IN THE FUTURE

God calls the festivals His **appointed times.** According to Strong's Concordance 4150, *mo'ed,* is translated **"appointed time"** and means **"a festival date."**

Speak to the sons of Israel and say to them, The Lord's APPOINTED TIMES which you shall proclaim as holy convocations—My APPOINTED TIMES are these. (Leviticus 23:2)

In the book of Daniel, the *time of indignation,* (synonym for "tribulation period"),[12] will occur at the **appointed time,** which can be interpreted that it will occur on a "festival date."

And he said, "Look, I am making known to you what shall happen in the latter TIME OF THE INDIGNATION; for at the APPOINTED TIME the end shall be. (Daniel 8:19)

All throughout the Bible, we see that important events occurred on festival dates. For example, both the Pharaoh of the Exodus, and Haman from the book of Esther, died on Aviv 17, which is the same date as the Festival of Firstfruits. The Festival of Firstfruits was when Yeshua rose from the dead. (This will be developed in the chapter on Firstfruits.) It was an **appointed time,** and I believe the symbolism is that the power of the resurrection is greater than the power of the enemy (symbolized by Pharaoh and Haman).

Years ago, a good friend of mine, Paula Benne, was told by God to celebrate the "Feast of Esther" on Easter Sunday that year. In obedience, she went to a beautiful hotel, read the book of Esther, and feasted at a fancy restaurant. Afterwards, when she told me the story, I asked her if she knew that the actual date she feasted (Easter Sunday) was the date of Esther's second banquet in the Bible. She had no idea and was amazed when she found out! I knew the date of Esther's banquet because of my study of the festivals. It was the same date as the resurrection (Easter Sunday) and the same date that Haman was hung on the gallows he had built for Esther's uncle Mordecai.

Paula and many others have been led on similar journeys that have paralleled festival dates. I love the fact that they didn't have knowledge of the festival dates or festival customs, but were led to walk into these God-ordained experiences!

Chapter 4

YESHUA AND THE EARLY CHURCH
CELEBRATED THE FESTIVALS

B y the time of Yeshua, there was a Temple and the festivals were being observed regularly. Yeshua's family went to Jerusalem every Passover. **(Luke 2:41)**

Yeshua was crucified as the Passover lamb after celebrating a Passover Seder meal with his disciples the night before. He told them them to continue to celebrate the festival in remembrance of Him. **(Luke 22:19, 1 Corinthians 11:24)**

Yeshua was actually crucified on the very day and time that the High Priest was slaying the sacrificial lamb in the Temple. Yeshua was the Lamb of God that was slain from the foundation of the earth.

Yeshua is *"the lamb that was,"* *"the lamb that is,"* and *"the lamb that is to come!"*

Knowing that ye were redeemed, not with corruptible things, with silver or gold, from your vain manner of life handed down from your fathers; but with precious blood, as of a lamb without spot, even the blood of Yeshua: who was FOREKNOWN

indeed before the foundation of the world, but was manifested at the end of times for your sake. (1 Peter 1:18-20)

Then I saw a Lamb, looking as if it had been slain, standing in the center of the throne, encircled by the four living creatures and the elders. (Revelation 5:6)

Yeshua attended *Sukkot*, also known as the "Feast of Tabernacles." **(John 7:2-14)** It was at this festival that He proclaimed He was the **living water** and the **light of the world.** Both of these expressions were associated with the particular customs of that festival. (This will be developed in the chapter on Sukkot.) By claiming to be the living water and the light of the world, some knew He was proclaiming to be the Messiah.

On hearing his words, some of the people said, "Surely this man is the Prophet." Others said, "He is the Messiah." (John 7:40-41)

Yeshua celebrated *Hanukkah*,[13] known as the "Feast of Dedication." **(John 10:22)**

The early Church was composed mainly of Jewish believers, and they continued to celebrate the festivals and attend synagogue as usual.

The New Covenant was instituted on the same date the disciples of Yeshua were celebrating the festival of *Shavuot* (Pentecost), which commemorated the *Giving of the Law* on Mount Sinai 1,500 years prior. (This will be developed in the chapter on *Shavuot*.)

In **Acts 12:3-4,** Herod Agrippa arrested Peter after the Festival of Unleavened Bread.

In **Acts 18:21,** Paul was debating with the Jews in Ephesus and they wanted him to stay longer. He refused and said, *"I must by all means keep this coming feast in Jerusalem."*

Paul sailed from Philippi after the Festival of Unleavened Bread. **(Acts 20:6)**

Paul wanted to be in Jerusalem by Pentecost. **(Acts 20:16)**

Acts 27:9 references "the Fast," which was referring to *Yom Kippur*, also known as the "Day of Atonement."

In **1 Corinthians 5:8,** Paul said *"Let us keep the festival."* In context, he was instructing the Corinthian believers on how to deal with an unrepentant man involved in sexual sin. Paul is comparing sin to leaven (yeast) and referencing the Festival of Unleavened Bread. In verse 7, he tells them that they are already unleavened (without sin) because Yeshua, the Passover lamb, had been sacrificed.

Faith in Yeshua was very widespread during the first century among the Jewish population. As more and more Gentiles were becoming believers, however, the Messianic communities began to radically change. After the death of the Apostle Paul in 66 CE, and when Rome attacked Jerusalem in 70 CE and destroyed the Temple, the believers scattered throughout the Roman Empire. Jewishness was seen as not being loyal to Rome and anti-Semitism began to be popular once more. This caused some of the spiritual communities to turn away from anything Jewish, especially in the second and third centuries. The Apostle Paul had warned that this would happen:

For I know this, after my departure savage wolves will come in among you, not sparing the flock. Also from among yourselves men will rise up, speaking perverse things, to draw away the disciples after themselves. (Acts 20:29-30)

Later, in the fourth century, Constantine, the Emperor of Rome, supposedly became a believer. In 325 CE, he convened the Council of Nicea. In this Council, he *purposely* left out every believing Jewish leader. Laws were passed that forbade Jewish believers to celebrate their festivals or to practice their customs. Pagan festivals were substituted for certain Biblical festivals. Greek names and concepts began to influence the faith. From then on, the Roman Julian Calendar, a solar calendar, was given precedence over the lunar Hebrew calendar.

When all of this happened, **many truths were lost** which are being restored in our day. For example, some teach that the doctrine of the rapture was a new doctrine, created in the 1800's. I do not believe that it was a new doctrine. I believe that it was an ancient truth that was lost and is being restored. I believe that the early Church, including the Apostle Paul, understood end-time theology because they understood what the festivals taught about the end-times. I believe they understood that the Spring festivals taught on Yeshua's First Coming and that the Fall festivals taught on His Second Coming.

The Apostle Paul wrote the following to the Thessalonian believers after a false teaching was circulating that **The Day of the Lord** had already come. He states that he doesn't need to write them about **times and dates,** and when this would occur, because they were already instructed in **times and dates** (the festivals).

But you have no need to have anything written to you, brothers, about the TIMES AND DATES when this will happen; because you yourselves well know that THE DAY OF THE LORD will come like a thief in the night. (1 Thessalonians 5:1-2)

I believe that the early Church understood that **The Day of the Lord** would begin on earth at the end of 6,000 years on the festival of Rosh Hashanah. I believe they knew that the *catching away* (rapture) would happen at the *last trump* (Rosh Hashanah) and a *false messiah* (antichrist) would arise at that time, and there would be a time of *birth pains* (tribulation period).

All of these concepts will be developed throughout this book.

Are you ready to go on an exciting voyage of discovery with me?

PART TWO: THE HEBRAIC CALENDAR

Chapter 5

THE TWO CALENDARS

In the beginning, God created time.
God called the light Day, and the darkness he called Night. So there was evening, and there was morning, one day. (Genesis 1:5)

The ancient Hebrews observed a twelve-month lunar calendar.

You made the moon to mark the seasons, and the sun knows when to set. (Psalms 104:19)

Our Western calendar is known as the Gregorian calendar and was instituted in 1582 by Pope Gregory XIII. Prior to this, the Julian calendar was in effect. These are solar calendars as they operate on the principle of the earth revolving around the sun.

The Hebraic calendar is a lunar calendar based on the movement of the moon around the earth. The dates of religious holidays are determined by the appearance of each new moon.

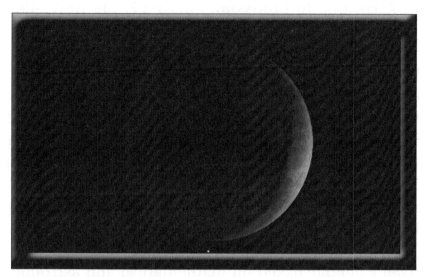

The lunar calendar is 10 days and 21 hours shorter than a solar year. To compensate, there is a periodic leap year in which a thirteenth month is added to the Hebraic calendar.

The Hebrews made sure that the Biblical festivals, known as the **appointed times** of the Lord, were observed on the correct days that God had instituted them. It was important to know the exact time of the New Moon. In ancient times, every month was determined by this observation.

The lunar month on the Jewish calendar begins when the first sliver of the moon becomes visible. When people observed the new moon, they would notify the Sanhedrin of Jerusalem (High Court composed of 70 elders) and they would declare *Rosh Chodesh* (first of the month). They would blow shofars, and light a chain of signal fires, and send out messengers to tell people when the new month began.

According to **Colossians 2:16-17,** the New Moon *(Rosh Chodesh)* was given to teach on things to come, and the substance would be about Yeshua. The sun can be a picture of Yeshua and the moon can be a picture of the believer. When the moon was being renewed at the beginning of the monthly cycle, it was said that it was being "born again." During the new moon phase, the moon only reflects a small portion of the sun's light. Each day as the moon turns toward the sun, it reflects more and more of the sun. So, it is with the believer as he turns toward Yeshua.

In the fourth century, Rabbi Hillel II established a fixed calendar based on mathematical and astronomical calculations. This calendar, still in use, standardized the length of months and the addition of months over the course of a 19-year cycle, so that the lunar calendar realigns with the solar years.

Having both a *solar* calendar and a *lunar* calendar can be very confusing. If that wasn't confusing enough, the Jewish people also have two different calendars, known as the *religious* and the *civil* calendars.

The **religious calendar** starts in the Spring (about March or April) in the month of Aviv (also called *Nisan*). The **civil calendar** starts in the Fall in the month of Tishri (about September or October).

The Jewish people have two concurrent calendar years. God established the new religious calendar when He brought them out of Egypt.

You are to begin your calendar with this month (Aviv); it will be the first month of the year for you. (Exodus 12:2)

Until that time, Aviv had been the seventh month on the civil calendar. Aviv would become the first month instead of Tishri, and Tishri would be the seventh month instead of Aviv.

The **civil calendar** is used in all passages of Scripture before Exodus 12. The **religious calendar** is used from Exodus 12 to Revelation 22.

One way to understand the concept of two Hebraic calendars, one religious and one civil, is to think of it like having two birthdays, your "natural" birthday and your "spiritual" birthday.

So, why is it important to know this information? There are numerous dates referenced in the Bible and you will need to know if the civil or religious calendar is being used.

For example, in **Genesis 8:4**, it tells us that Noah's ark rested in the seventh month, on the seventeenth day of the month, upon the mountains of Ararat. Since this is before **Exodus 12**, you would look at the civil calendar. The seventh month on the civil calendar is Aviv. So, the ark settled on Mt. Ararat on the 17th of Aviv. This is an important date throughout the Scriptures. (As referenced earlier, it's the same date that both Pharaoh and Haman were killed, and it's the same date that Yeshua rose from the dead.) Noah's ark rested on Mt. Ararat on the same day as the resurrection of Yeshua, and could be symbolic of a "new beginning."

When you understand the two calendars, you can understand why Yeshua's two appearances, at the time known as the *former rain* (Spring festivals) and the time known as the *latter rain* (Fall festivals) can both be in the **first month** as referenced in **Joel 2:23**. There are two first months – one in the Spring (Aviv) and one in the Fall (Tishri)!

Be glad then, you children of Zion, and rejoice in the Lord your God; For He has given you the former rain faithfully, and He will cause the rain to come down for you— The FORMER RAIN, and the LATTER RAIN in the FIRST MONTH. (Joel 2:23)

Civil Calendar
1. Tishri (Ethanim)
2. Cheshvan (Bul)
3. Kislev
4. Tevet
5. Sh'vat
6. Adar
7. Aviv (Nisan)
8. Iyar (Zif)
9. Sivan
10. Tammuz
11. Av
12. Elul

Religious Calendar
1. Aviv (Nisan)
2. Iyar (Zif)
3. Sivan
4. Tammuz
5. Av
6. Elul
7. Tishri (Ethanim)
8. Chesvan (Bul)
9. Kislev

10. Tevet
11. Sh'vat
12. Adar

The Festival Dates (Religious Calendar)

1. Pesach/Passover	Aviv 14
2. Hag haMatzah/Unleavened Bread	Aviv 15-21
3. Firstfruits of the Barley Harvest	Day after Sabbath During Hag haMatzah
4. Shavuot/Pentecost	50 Days After Firstfruits
5. Rosh Hashanah/Trumpets	Tishri 1
6. Yom Kippur/Atonement	Tishri 10
7. Sukkot/Tabernacles	Tishri 15-21

Chapter 6

THE 7,000–YEAR PLAN OF GOD

In addition to understanding the Hebraic calendar, one needs to comprehend God's "7,000-year plan." Never heard of this before? I'll walk you through it.

God could have finished Creation in a moment of time, but instead He created it in six, 24-hour days. He rested on the seventh day and instituted *Shabbat,* or "Sabbath" (meaning rest).

God was revealing to us his blueprint for the ages and teaching us about the Messianic Kingdom and the Age to Come.

The Bible states that a day can be likened to a thousand years.

A thousand years in your sight are like a day that has just gone by. (Psalms 90:4)

Moreover, dear friends, do not ignore this: with the Lord, one day is like a thousand years and a thousand years like one day. (2 Peter 3:8)

In the apocryphal[14] Epistle of Barnabas,[15] it's stated that the end of time will happen at the end of 6,000 years, and that the seventh day will be the time of rest (known as the millennium), and the eighth day is eternity.

*Epistle of Barnabas 15:3-5, 9: He speaks of the Sabbath at the beginning of the Creation, "And God made in six days the works of His hands and on the seventh day He made an end, and rested in it and sanctified it." Notice, children, what is the meaning of "He made an end in six days?" He means this: that the Lord will make **an end of everything in six thousand years**, for a day with Him means a thousand years.*

And He Himself is my witness when He says, "Lo, the day of the Lord shall be as a thousand years." So then, children, in six days, that is in six thousand years, everything will be completed. "And He rested on the seventh day." This means, when His Son comes He will destroy the time of the wicked one, and will judge the godless, and will change the sun and the moon and the stars, and then He will truly rest on the seventh day.

Verse 9: When resting from all things I shall begin the eighth day, that is, the beginning of the other world.

Yeshua came into the world at the end of 4,000 years. I believe He will return at the end of 6,000 years and there will be 1,000 years of rest on earth (known as the millennium). We will then experience the *eighth day*, which is known as "eternity."

The Apostle John, an observant Jew, wrote the following after being exiled to an island called Patmos in the first century:

And I saw an angel coming down out of heaven, having the key of the abyss and a great chain in his hand. And he laid hold on the dragon, the old serpent, which is the Devil and Satan, and bound him for A

THOUSAND YEARS, and cast him into the abyss, and shut it, and sealed it over him, that he should deceive the nations no more, until THE THOUSAND YEARS should be finished: after this he must be loosed for a little time. (Revelation 20:1-3)

We see several types and shadows of the 7,000-year plan of God in the Scriptures. For example, in **Matthew 17:1-4**, we read that Yeshua went up on a high mountain **after six days.** (Remember a day is as a thousand years–I believe there is a hidden message here.) I believe this was the festival of *Sukkot*, also known as the "Feast of Tabernacles," which teaches on the Messianic Kingdom to come that will take place at the end of 6,000 years. *Why do I believe this?* Because Moses and Elijah appeared and Peter offered to build them three tabernacles (temporary structures that are built at the festival of Sukkot.) We'll look at this again in the chapter on *Sukkot* (Feast of Tabernacles).

In **2 Kings 11**, we read that Joash was hidden for **six years** while the evil Athaliah (type of Satan) ruled the land. In the **seventh year**, he was crowned as king. I believe that the coronation of the rightful king at the end of **six years** corresponds to Yeshua's coronation at the end of six thousand years. The coronation theme will be developed further in the chapter on Rosh Hashanah (Feast of Trumpets).

In the first two chapters of John's Gospel, we see that Yeshua attended a wedding on the **seventh day.** The first four days are found in v. 19, 29, 35, and 43 of Chapter One. On the **fourth day**, Yeshua travels and is not seen again until the **seventh day** in Chapter 2. Since it has been established that **a day is as a thousand**

years, I believe this is a hidden message showing the overall plan of God. The **seventh day**, the day of Yeshua's return, is the millennium.

These are only a few of the many types and shadows, and layers of understanding, that we see throughout the Bible showing a picture of the 7,000-year plan of God.

Chapter 7

THE DAY OF THE LORD

The Day of the Lord is the "seventh day" in the Bible and is referred to more than 300 times in Scripture. It is one of the most important themes of the entire Bible. I believe that this term is referring to the millennium (which includes the seven years of the tribulation period).

The article entitled *Millennium* from **The Encyclopedia of the Jewish Religion,** edited by R.J. Awi Werblowsky and Georffrey Wigoder, 1986 by Adama Books, page 263, states the belief that each day of the week of Creation represented a one thousand year day of God, with the seventh day being **The Day of the Lord,** or millennium.

Here are some verses referencing **The Day of the Lord**:

Blow the trumpet in Zion, and sound an alarm in My holy mountain! Let all the inhabitants of the land tremble; For THE DAY OF THE LORD is coming, For it is at hand: a day of darkness and gloominess, a day of clouds and thick darkness. (Joel 2:1-2)

Woe to you who desire THE DAY OF THE LORD! For what good is THE DAY OF THE LORD to you? It will be darkness, and not light. (Amos 5:18)

For you yourselves know perfectly that THE DAY OF THE LORD so comes as a thief in the night. For when they say, "Peace and safety!" then sudden destruction comes upon them, as labor pains upon a pregnant woman. And they shall not escape. (1 Thessalonians 5:2-3)

For those who experience the tribulation period on earth, it will be a day of darkness and gloom as the wrath of God is being poured out.

For THE GREAT DAY OF HIS WRATH has come, and who is able to stand? (Revelation 6:17)

Then I saw another sign in heaven, great and marvelous: seven angels having the seven last plagues, for in them THE WRATH OF GOD is complete. (Revelation 15:7)

I believe that those who are righteous will not experience this wrath of God on earth, but will be sheltered during this time.

Come, my people, enter your rooms, and shut your doors behind you. Hide yourselves for a little while until THE WRATH is past. For see! The Lord emerges from his place to punish those on earth for their sin. (Isaiah 26:21-22)

For God did not appoint us to WRATH, but to obtain salvation through our Lord Jesus Christ. (1 Thessalonians 5:9)

We're told to look forward to **The Day of the Lord. (2 Peter 3:14)** It will not be a day of darkness and gloom for the righteous. I believe that the Scriptures teach that the righteous will be hidden during the time of the tribulation period, and will return to earth at the end of that seven-year period to live out the rest of the millennium on earth. This theme will be developed fully in the chapters on the Fall festivals.

Other Titles for The Day of the Lord:

- The Day of the Lord of Hosts **(Isaiah 2:12)**
- The Day of Punishment **(Isaiah 10:3)**
- The Day of His Fierce Anger **(Lamentations 1:12)**
- The Day the Lord Gives You Rest **(Isaiah 14:3)**
- The Day of Grief and Desperate Sorrow **(Isaiah 17:11)**
- A Day of Trouble **(Isaiah 22:5 and Ezekiel 7:7)**
- The Day of the East Wind **(Isaiah 27:8)**
- The Day of the Great Slaughter **(Isaiah 30:25)**
- A Day of Trouble and Rebuke and Blasphemy **(Isaiah 37:3, 2 Kings 19:3)**
- The Day of Salvation **(Isaiah 49:8)**
- The Day of Vengeance **(Isaiah 61:2, Isaiah 63:4, Jeremiah 46:10, Proverbs 6:34)**
- The Day of Slaughter **(Jeremiah 12:3)**
- The Day of Affliction **(Jeremiah 16:19)**
- The Day of Evil **(Jeremiah 17:17, 18, Amos 6:3)**
- The Day of Trouble **(Jeremiah 51:2)**
- The Day of Destruction **(Job 21:30)**

- The Day of Their Calamity **(Jeremiah 18:17, Jeremiah 46:21, Deuteronomy 32:35)**
- The Day of the Lord God of Hosts **(Jeremiah 46:10)**
- The Day You Have Announced **(Lamentations 1:21)**
- The Day of His Anger **(Lamentations 2:1)**
- The Day We Have Waited For **(Lamentations 7:16)**
- The Day of Your Anger **(Lamentations 2:21)**
- The Day of the Lord's Anger **(Lamentations 2:22, Zephaniah 2:2, 3)**
- The Day of the Wrath of the Lord **(Ezekiel 7:19)**
- The Day **(Ezekiel 30:2,3, Joel 1:15, Malachi 4:1, 1 Corinthians 3:13)**
- A Day of Clouds **(Ezekiel 30:3)**
- The Day of Egypt **(Ezekiel 30:9)**
- The Day of Your Fall **(Ezekiel 32.10)**
- The Day That I Am Glorified **(Ezekiel 39:13)**
- The Day of Jezreel **(Hosea 1:11)**
- The Day of Rebuke **(Hosea 5:9)**
- The Day of Our King **(Hosea 7:5)**
- The Appointed Day **(Hosea 9:5)**
- The Day of The Feast of the Lord **(Hosea 9:5)**
- The Days of Punishment **(Hosea 9:7)**
- The Days of Recompense **(Hosea 9:7)**
- The Day of Darkness and Gloominess **(Joel 2:2, Zephaniah 1:15)**
- A Day of Clouds and Thick Darkness **(Joel 2:2, Zephaniah 1:15)**
- The Great and Terrible Day of the Lord **(Joel 2:31)**

- The Day of Battle **(Amos 1:14, Zechariah 14:3, Psalms 140:7, Proverbs 21:31)**
- The Day of the Whirlwind **(Amos 1:14)**
- The Day of Trouble **(Nahum 1:7, Habakkuk 3:16, Psalms 50:15)**
- The Day of Jacob's Trouble **(Jeremiah 30:7)**
- The Great Day of the Lord **(Zephaniah 1:14)**
- A Day of Wrath **(Zephaniah 1:15)**
- A Day of Trouble and Distress **(Zephaniah 1:15)**
- The Day of Wrath **(Job 21:30, Proverbs 11:4)**
- The Day of Your Power **(Psalms 110:3)**
- The Day of Adversity **(Proverbs 24:10)**
- The Day of His Espousals **(Song of Solomon 3:11)**
- The Day of the Gladness of His Heart **(Song of Solomon 3:11)**
- A Day on Which He Will Judge the World in Righteousness by Whom He Had Ordained **(Acts 17:31)**
- The Day the Lord Binds Up the Bruise of His People **(Isaiah 30:26)**

Chapter 8

Pesach (Passover)

הַפֶּסַח

Pesach, or "Passover," is the first of the seven *moedim*, or **"appointed times,"** listed in Leviticus 23.

On the fourteenth day of the first month at twilight is the Lord's Passover. (Leviticus 23:5)

This month is referred to as Aviv (or Nisan). The month of Aviv comes in the Spring (April or May on the Gregorian calendar). This month is the first month on the religious calendar.

Once settled in the Promised Land, all Jewish males were able to obey the commandment to go to Jerusalem *"to appear before the Lord"* for this festival. **(Deuteronomy 16:16)** It commemorates the Exodus from Egypt on this date. It was at this festival that Yeshua was crucified as the Passover lamb.

John saw Yeshua coming toward him, and said, "Behold! The Lamb of God who takes away the sin of the world!" (John 1:29)

For 3,500 years, since the days of Moses, Jewish people all over the world have celebrated the festival of Passover. The Hebrew name *Pesach* means "to pass over, exempt, or spare." It refers to the fact that God "passed over" and protected the houses of the Jews when the firstborn of Egypt were being slain.

Pesach (Passover) is one of the most commonly observed Jewish holidays, even by otherwise non-religious Jews. Each year the Jewish people celebrate the first night of this holiday with a Seder meal. The word *Seder* means "set order" as there are 15 steps to the meal that follow a specific order. A traditional Seder can take four or five hours. TThe 15 steps are found in a book called a *haggadah,*[16] that is found at each setting at the table. Each of the 15 steps of the Seder correspond to the 15 literal steps in the Temple where the Levites would ascend, taking them closer to the Holy of Holies. Each step of the Seder is designed to help those participating ascend into the presence of God.

Everything in the Passover Seder points to Yeshua, who celebrated the Seder with His disciples the evening before His crucifixion, which is commonly called "The Last Supper." Leonardo da Vinci's famous painting of "The Last Supper" is not accurate because it depicts leavened bread. Absolutely no leaven is permitted at this meal or in people's homes during this season.

For 1,500 years before Yeshua's First Coming, the ritual of slaying lambs at Pesach (Passover) was conducted. Yeshua fulfilled every detail of the *mo'ed* (appointment) as He was our Passover lamb. He was crucified on the **exact** day, month, and hour that the High Priest would slay the lamb in the Temple.

Knowing that you were not redeemed with corruptible things...but with the precious blood of Yeshua, as of a lamb without blemish and without spot. (1 Peter 1:18-19)

The story of the first Passover is told in Exodus, chapters 1 to 15. For many years, the Children of Israel had been in bitter slavery to the Pharaohs in Egypt. They cried out for deliverance, and God sent Moses as a deliverer. Moses appeared before the Pharaoh many times and challenged him to let God's people "go." Each time the Pharaoh agreed, but went back on his promise. At each refusal, God sent a plague on the land of Egypt. After the ninth refusal, God promised a final judgment on Egypt.

God provided redemption by commanding every household to take a lamb without spot or blemish, kill it, and pour its blood into a basin. With a hyssop plant, they were to strike the blood on each doorpost and the top of the lintel or crosspiece.

The last plague was that the firstborn son in every house in Egypt would die. Those that had the blood at their door were promised that God Himself would ***pass over*** their houses to protect them. After this plague, the Pharaoh finally let the people go and this began the exodus to the Promised Land.

Egypt can be a type of the ungodly world system and the Pharaoh can be a type of Satan. We are delivered from both, through the applied blood of Yeshua. Just as the Pharaoh did not want to let the Children of Israel go, Satan does not want to let us go. Just as the Children of Israel had to possess the Promised Land, we must possess the promises of God.

After the Temple was built, Jews traveled to Jerusalem to celebrate Passover as they were commanded. Yeshua's parents traveled to Jerusalem yearly to celebrate Passover. When Yeshua was 12, He amazed the religious teachers with His understanding at this festival. **(Luke 2:41-50)**

Every household was to inspect the lamb for four days before Passover to make sure it was perfect in every way. Yeshua entered Jerusalem four days before His crucifixion and was examined before the religious leaders who could not find a flaw in Him. **(John 19:4)**

In the temple, at 9:00 am on the 14th day of Aviv, a lamb was tied to the horns of the altar. This was the day and the hour that Yeshua was nailed to the cross. **(Mark 15:25)**

At 3:00 pm, the High Priest would slit the lamb's throat and say, "*It is finished!*" This is the same time that Yeshua died with His last words being **"*It is finished.*" (John 19:30)**

In preparing the lamb for the Passover meal, the book of Exodus commanded that the bones of the lamb could not be broken. Yeshua's legs were not broken to hasten death as was the custom at crucifixion. **(John 19:33)**

After the Temple was destroyed in 70 CE, the Jews were further dispersed to many nations, but still continued to celebrate Pesach (Passover)–even to this day. They started to use a shank bone of a lamb on the Seder plate to represent the original sacrifice of the lambs. Yeshua's one sacrifice atoned for all sins of all time, making any further sacrifice unnecessary.

And every priest stands ministering daily and offering repeatedly the same sacrifices, which can never take away sins. But this Man, after He had offered one sacrifice for sins forever, sat down at the right hand of God. (Hebrews 10:11-12)

In each home, they were instructed to roast the lambs on a wooden spit. The intestines were to be taken out and put around the lamb's head. They called the lamb a **crowned sacrifice.** (The wooden spit resembled the cross that Yeshua was crucified on while wearing a **crown of thorns.** This was hundreds of years before the Romans introduced crucifixion.) Coincidence? I don't think so!

The customs and traditions for this festival come from the Torah (the five books of Moses) and the Talmud. The Talmud is a central text in Judaism and consists of 63 tractates or essays and is over 6,200 pages long. It contains the Oral Law known as the Mishnah and also the collective opinions of thousands of rabbis on a variety of subjects over centuries past.

There are four glasses of wine that are drunk during the course of the Seder. (*You may need a designated driver if you have a low tolerance to alcohol!*) Wine is a symbol of joy and thanksgiving. It also represents the blood of Yeshua to Messianic Jews and Christians.

The first cup is called the *cup of blessing* or *sanctification*. The second is the *cup of judgment* or *affliction*. The third is the *cup of redemption*. The fourth is the *cup of praise* or *restoration*.

The four cups are thought to represent the four-part promise that the Lord made to the Children of Israel found in **Exodus 6:** *"I will bring you out; I will deliver you from bondage; I will redeem you with an outstretched arm; and I will take you to Me for a people."*

At most Seders, everyone who participates ceremoniously washes and dries his or her hands. This symbolizes the High Priest who washed before entering the Holy of Holies. At His last Passover Seder with His 12 disciples, Yeshua took this time to teach them a lesson in humility as He washed their feet.

Let's look at some of the symbols on the Seder plate:
- A **shank bone** of a lamb. Since the destruction of the Temple, typically lamb of any kind is not eaten at Passover. The shank bone is a reminder

of the lamb. It is called the *zeroah*, which is Hebrew for "arm."

And remember that you were a slave in the land of Egypt, and the Lord your God brought you out from there by a mighty hand and by an outstretched ARM. (Deuteronomy 5:15)

- A **roasted egg** has been added to the Seder plate since the time of Yeshua. The egg is regarded as a symbol of mourning, reminding Jews of the destruction of the Temple. One legend says that just as the egg gets hard as it cooks, so the Jewish people grow harder as tyrants throughout history have tried to annihilate them. It may also symbolize the hardness of the Pharaoh's heart.

- The next symbol is the **bitter herbs**. Lettuce in the Middle East was bitter as it stayed in the ground for a long time. Horseradish is also a bitter herb. The bitter herbs are symbolic of the Children of Israel's slavery in Egypt. Messianic Jews and Christians believe it can represent the bitter cup that Yeshua drank on our behalf.

- Another symbol is **charoset**, a mixture of apples, nuts, spices, and wine. This can represent the mortar the Children of Israel used to make bricks in Egypt. The mixture is sweet and is eaten with bitter herbs to remind participants in the Seder that even the most bitter of circumstances can be sweetened if there is hope in God. It is made from the fruit found in the Promised Land and reminds the participant of the promises of God.

- The **parsley** represents the hyssop that was used in Egypt to apply the blood to the doorposts. It also represents life because of its green color. A sprig of parsley is dipped in **salt water** and eaten. The salt water represents tears, as life in Egypt was a life of pain and suffering.

There are three matzos on the table commemorating the unleavened bread that the Hebrews ate in their hasty departure from Egypt. They are placed in a bag with three compartments called a *matzah tash* or "unity bag." The middle piece of matzah is removed and broken in half during the meal. It is then wrapped in a linen napkin and hidden (buried) under a pillow of something soft. The children close their eyes when it is hidden. It will be found (resurrected) later by one of them and they will negotiate for a gift.

The three matzos can represent the Father, the Son, and the Holy Spirit. The middle piece would represent Yeshua, who was broken and wrapped in linen, hidden in a tomb, and then resurrected. The broken piece of matzah that is hidden is called the *afikoman*, which means, "I came" in Greek.

Some rabbis teach that the three matzos represent the three patriarchs: Abraham, Isaac, and Jacob. However the question arises, "*Why break Isaac?*"

The retelling of the story of the first Passover takes place during the Seder. This begins with the youngest person asking a set of four questions:

1. *On all other nights,* we eat bread and matzah. On this night, why do we eat only matzah?
2. *On all other nights,* we eat all kinds of vegetables. On this night, why do we eat only bitter herbs?

3. *On all other nights*, we do not dip our vegetables even once. On this night, why do we dip them twice?

4. *On all other nights,* we eat our meals sitting. On this night, why do we eat only reclining?

It is believed to be both a duty and a privilege to answer the four questions of Passover and to recite the mighty works of our faithful God.

And you shall tell your son in that day, saying, 'This is done because of what the Lord did for me when I came up from Egypt.' It shall be as a sign to you on your hand and as a memorial between your eyes, that the Lord's law may be in your mouth; for with a strong hand the Lord has brought you out of Egypt. You shall therefore keep this ordinance in its season from year to year. (Exodus 13:8-10)

A rabbi by the name of Hillel, in the first century, created a custom of making a finger sandwich with the *matzos* ("unleavened bread") and the *maror* ("bitter herbs") to fulfill **Exodus 12:8,** which says matzah will be eaten with maror. A sandwich is made by placing the horseradish on one side of the matzah and the *charoset* (apple mixture) on the other. The horseradish burns your mouth and brings tears to your eyes. You have to keep eating until you get to the charoset, the sweetness, which is the antidote to the horseradish. This symbolizes the hard times in life and how we keep pressing on until we obtain the promises of God, which are sweet.

A festive meal is eaten during the Seder. Favorites are gefilte fish, matzah ball soup, and roasted chicken.

It's one of the most delicious meals of the year. The meal must end long before midnight to allow the afikoman to be located and eaten before that hour.

The *afikoman* (the piece of matzah that was hidden earlier) is eaten as a dessert. There are different traditions relating to this, but most parents hide it and the child who finds it negotiates for a small gift or money. The Seder cannot continue without it. The gift that is given later is sometimes called **the promise of the Father.**

And gathering them together, He commanded them that they should not depart from Jerusalem, but wait for THE PROMISE OF THE FATHER, which, He said, ye have heard of Me. (Acts 1:4)

I believe that the afikoman was the piece of matzah where Yeshua said *"this is My body given for you; this do in remembrance of Me."* Yeshua told his disciples that they would be given *"the promise of the Father,"* the Holy Spirit, after his resurrection. The fact that it has to be found and eaten before midnight is very significant as we're told that the Bridegroom will return at midnight.

And at midnight a cry was heard: 'Behold, the bridegroom is coming; go out to meet him! (Matthew 25:6)

The Seder ends with participants joyfully shouting, *"Next Year in Jerusalem!"* As believers in Messiah, we hope to celebrate in the heavenly **New Jerusalem.**

Today, there is an extra place setting at the Seder table, as it has been for hundreds of years. This place setting is for Elijah, the prophet, who was expected to come at Passover to proclaim the coming Messiah.

Elijah did not see death, but was swept up to heaven in a whirlwind–in a chariot of fire.

Before John the Baptist's birth, the angel Gabriel said to his soon-to-be father, *"And he will go before the Lord, in the spirit and power of Elijah...to make ready a people prepared for the Lord." (Luke 1:17)*

It can be figured out mathematically, that *John the Baptist was born at Passover!* According to Yeshua, John was the Elijah to come!

And if you are willing to receive it, he (John) is Elijah who is to come. (Matthew 11:14)

The last verses in the *Tanach* (Hebrew for what is known as the Old Testament) are:

Behold, I will send you Elijah the prophet before the coming of the great and dreadful day of the Lord. And he will turn the hearts of the fathers to the children, and the hearts of the children to their fathers, lest I come and strike the earth with a curse. (Malachi 4:5-6)

Yeshua said that John the Baptist was the greatest prophet that ever lived, but he who is least in the Kingdom is greater than John.

For I say to you, among those born of women there is not a greater prophet than John the Baptist; but he who is least in the kingdom of God is greater than he. (Luke 7:28)

Many believe and teach that John the Baptist doubted that Yeshua was the Messiah. This mistaken idea comes from the question John asked when he was in prison:

And when John had heard in prison about the works of Yeshua, he sent two of his disciples and said to Him, "Are You the Coming One, or do we look for another?" (Matthew 11:2-3)

The reason John posed the question was because of a first century rabbinical teaching of two separate Messiahs. When Jewish scholars and rabbis studied about the Messiah, they found that certain passages seemed to contradict one another. Often the Messiah was seen as a **conquering king (Zechariah 14, Psalms 2, Isaiah 63-66, Jeremiah 23),** yet other passages depicted him as a **suffering servant (Isaiah 40-53 and 61, Psalms 22, and Daniel 9).** John asked the question whether Yeshua was the Messiah (indicating one, singular) or if they were to expect another – *a second one.*

I do not believe that John the Baptist doubted that Yeshua was the Messiah. John had recognized Him while He was still in his mother's womb. **(Luke 1:41)** It was John's mandate to identify and prepare the way for Yeshua as the Lamb of God that came to take away the sin of the world. **(John 1:29)**

I believe his question was specifically whether Yeshua would fulfill all of the prophecies concerning the Messiah, or whether there would be a second Messiah coming. Yeshua's answer **(Matthew 11:4-6)** was a paraphrase of various passages that referred to *Messiah ben Joseph* (**suffering servant**) and *Messiah ben David* (**conquering king**). He was answering that He would fulfill all of the Messianic prophecies.

Rather than send two different Messiahs, God would send one Messiah in two separate appearances. The prophecies of the suffering servant would be fulfilled in the First Coming and the prophecies of the conquering king would be fulfilled in a Second Coming.

Chapter 9

HAG HAMATZAH (UNLEAVENED BREAD)

האזתאמאה גאה

In Leviticus 23, *Hag haMatzah* is also known as the "Festival of Unleavened Bread." It is mentioned as a separate festival and starts the day after Passover.

The Lord's Passover begins at twilight on the fourteenth day of the first month. On the fifteenth day of that month the Lord's FESTIVAL OF UNLEAVENED BREAD begins; for seven days you must eat bread made without yeast. (Leviticus 23:5-6)

Throughout the book of John, the Passover refers not only to Aviv 14 (the actual date of Passover) but also to the eight days that include the Festival of Unleavened Bread.

The Lord said that for seven days the Children of Israel must eat *matzos*, which is "unleavened bread." This bread was made without yeast when the Lord brought them out of Egypt in haste.

In Scripture, leaven can represent sin. It is forbidden to have even a crumb of leavened bread in the house during this festival.

Several weeks prior to this holiday, religious Jews do a thorough cleaning to rid the home of all leaven. *Perhaps this is where the custom of spring-cleaning originated?*

On the night before Passover, in Orthodox Jewish homes, the father takes a candle and does a final search for any remaining leaven in the house. Traditionally, he sweeps breadcrumbs that the mother purposely hid throughout the house onto a wooden spoon using a feather. Next, the leaven is wrapped in a cloth and cast out the door as the father recites the appropriate blessing. The following morning, the father picks up the cloth and goes to their synagogue and burns it.

Could this be a picture of salvation?

The candle can represent the Word of God, which is often referred to as light, revealing the sin in our lives. The leavened bread could represent sin and it is swept onto the wooden spoon that could represent the wooden cross. The feather could represent the Holy Spirit as He appeared in the form of a dove. You know, just having the Word is not enough–the Holy Spirit must reveal it and its mysteries.

I believe that the Christian tradition of communion is taken from the Jewish Passover Seder. We are told to examine ourselves for hidden sin before taking the bread and wine during communion.

Everyone ought to examine him or herself before they eat of the bread and drink from the cup. (1 Corinthians 11:28).

In some Christian congregations, "Good Friday" is celebrated as the day Yeshua was crucified. Actually, Yeshua had to be crucified on a Thursday in order for

Him to be in the ground three days and three nights and to rise on the first day of the week (Sunday).

For as Jonah was three days and three nights in the belly of the great fish, so will the Son of Man be three days and three nights in the heart of the earth. (Matthew 12:40)

Now on the first day of the week (Sunday) Mary Magdalene went to the tomb early, while it was still dark, and saw that the stone had been taken away from the tomb. (John 20:1)

So, why do we celebrate the crucifixion on "Good Friday" if Yeshua was actually crucified on a Thursday?

The confusion is because the Church, for the most part, does not understand festival language or Hebraic customs. The confusion stems from **John 19:31**, that states Yeshua's body had to be taken down from the cross because the next day was the Sabbath. The first day of the Festival of Unleavened Bread is considered a *Shabbaton* (a high Sabbath). This verse wasn't referring to the weekly Sabbath (Friday at Sundown to Saturday at Sundown), but to the high Sabbath that was on Friday, Aviv 15, that year.

There are different types of leaven we are told to *avoid* in the Scriptures.

1. The **leaven of Herod,** which can represent the political spirit or worldliness. **(Mark 8:14-15, 6:14-18, and Matthew 2:7-12)**
2. The **leaven of the Pharisees** that can represent hypocrisy. **(Matthew 16:5-12; 23:1-3; Luke 11:37-44; 12:1)**

3. The **leaven of the Sadducees**, which can represent false doctrine. The Sadducees did not believe in the supernatural and denied the existence of angels and the resurrection. **(Mark 12:18; Acts 23:6-8)**

4. The **leaven of Corinth,** which can represent sensuality (fornication). **(1 Corinthians 4:17-21; 5:1-13; 6:1; 9-11, 13, 16-18; 8:1; 13:4; 2 Corinthians 12:20-21)**

5. The **leaven of Galatia,** which can represent legalism. **(Galatians 5:9)**

In the past, godly kings and leaders in Israel always brought the people back to keeping the festivals of Passover and Unleavened Bread. **(2 Chronicles 8:12-13; 2 Chronicles 30:13-21; 35:17-19; Ezra 6:19-22; Ezekiel 45:21)**

Unleavened bread was used in the consecration of priests to their office and ministry. **(Leviticus 8:1-2, 26-27; Exodus 29:1-2, 23)** It was used in the sacred vow of separation of the Nazarite to the Lord. **(Numbers 6:13-21)** Unleavened bread was used when Gideon was called into service. **(Judges 6:17-24)**

It was at this festival season that Yeshua drove the greedy moneychangers out of the Temple. I believe He was purging His Father's house of *leaven* (sin).

Now the Passover of the Jews was at hand, and Yeshua went up to Jerusalem. And He found in the Temple those who sold oxen and sheep and doves, and the moneychangers doing business. When He had made a whip of cords, He drove them all out of the temple, with the sheep and the oxen, and poured

out the changers' money and overturned the tables. And He said to those who sold doves, "Take these things away! Do not make My Father's house a house of merchandise! (John 2:13-16)

In understanding the Festival of Unleavened Bread, it helps us to understand this exhortation from the Apostle Paul as he challenges the Corinthian Church to deal with sexual sin in their midst.

Do you not know that a little leaven leavens the whole lump? Therefore purge out the old leaven, that you may be a new lump, since you truly are unleavened. For indeed Yeshua, our Passover, was sacrificed for us. Therefore let us keep the feast, not with old leaven, nor with the leaven of malice and wickedness, but with the unleavened bread of sincerity and truth. (1 Corinthians 5:6-8)

Could the matzah itself be a picture of Yeshua?

It is without leaven like Yeshua was without sin. Matzah is **striped** and **pierced** during baking. Yeshua was *"pierced for our transgressions"* and *"by His stripes we are healed."* **(Isaiah 53)**

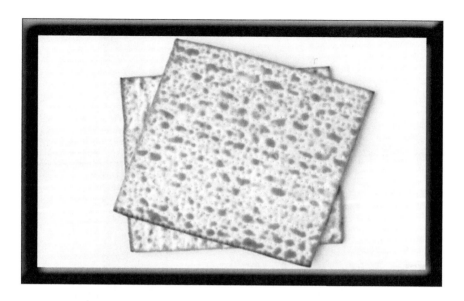

Yeshua identified Himself as the **bread of life.**

And Yeshua said to them, I am the bread of life. He who comes to Me shall never hunger (John 6:35)

Yeshua also identified Himself as the **living bread** that came down from heaven, which a man may eat of and live forever.

I am the LIVING BREAD that came down from heaven. If anyone eats of this bread, he will live forever (John 6:51)

Chapter 10

FIRSTFRUITS

סְתָרְשׁתסרשׁ

The Festival of Firstfruits occurs during the week of the Festival of Unleavened Bread on the day after the weekly Sabbath (which begins at sundown on Friday and ends at sundown on Saturday). In other words, it is the first Sunday after the 15th of Aviv.

And the Lord spoke to Moses, saying, "Speak to the children of Israel, and say to them: 'when you come into the land which I give to you, and reap its harvest, then you shall bring a sheaf of the firstfruits of your harvest to the priest. He shall wave the sheaf before the Lord, to be accepted on your behalf; on THE DAY AFTER THE SABBATH the priest shall wave it. (Leviticus 23:9-11)

God commanded the people, once they entered the Promised Land, to bring the firstfruits of their barley harvest as a wave offering before Him on that day.

Once in the Promised Land, barley was the first grain to ripen. A man would go to the standing harvest, take a sheaf of barley and bring the sheaf of firstfruits to the priest. The priest would wave the sheaf before the Lord.

Yeshua was resurrected on this date, Aviv 17, which was the Festival of Firstfruits.

But now Messiah is risen from the dead, and has become the FIRSTFRUITS of those who have fallen asleep. For as in Adam all die, so also in Messiah shall all be made alive. But each in his own order: Yeshua the FIRSTFRUITS; then they that are Yeshua's, at His coming. (1 Corinthians 15:20, 22-23)

The people were forbidden to use any part of the harvest until after the firstfruits were offered to the Lord.

You shall eat neither bread nor parched grain nor fresh grain until the same day that you have brought an offering to your God; it shall be a statute forever throughout your generations in all your dwellings. (Leviticus 23:14)

Other prescribed offerings were also presented on this day. In one of the Temple courts, the grain was threshed, and then parched over an open flame, and winnowed in the wind to remove the chaff. The barley was then milled and put through an intensive sifting process until sifted very fine.

On the morning of Aviv 17, the firstfruits were presented to the Lord. One *omer* (about "five pints") of the barley flour was mixed with ¾ pint of olive oil, and a small amount of frankincense was sprinkled on it. This became the firstfruits offering. The priest would wave it before the Lord and burn a small amount on the altar. The remainder was given to the Levites.

Each family also brought their firstfruits offering to the Temple as well. As they did, Levitical choirs would sing **Psalms 30**.

Sheaves can be representative of people. Young Joseph dreamed that eleven sheaves bowed down to his sheaf. The interpretation was that the sheaves represented his brothers.

Psalms 126 speaks of the sower–sowing in tears but reaping in joy, bringing his sheaves with him. This could be applied to Yeshua. He is the Lord of the Harvest and there will be a great harvest at the end of the age. **(Matthew 13:39)**

Firstfruits were always the first and the best. The concept of firstfruits is a major theme in the Bible.

- Yeshua was the **firstborn** of Mary. **(Matthew 1:23-25)**
- Yeshua was the **first begotten** of God the Father. **(Hebrews 1:6)**
- Yeshua was the **firstborn** over all Creation. **(Colossians 1:15)**
- Yeshua was the **first begotten** from the dead. **(Revelation 1:5)**

- Yeshua was the **firstborn** of many brethren. **(Romans 8:29)**
- Yeshua is the **firstfruits** of the resurrected ones.
- **(1 Corinthians 15:20, 23)**
- Yeshua is the **preeminent** One. **(Colossians 1:18)**

The principle of giving our **firstfruits** to the Lord comes with a promise.

Honor the Lord with your possessions, and with the FIRSTFRUITS of all your increase, so your barns will be filled with plenty, and your vats will overflow with new wine. (Proverbs 3:9-10)

Since the Temple was destroyed in 70 CE, firstfruits sacrifices and offerings are no longer offered the same way they were in ancient times. This date is now used to count the days to the next festival. It is known as the **"Counting of the Omer."** The Children of Israel were told to count 49 days from Firstfruits and the 50th day is known *Shavuot* or *Pentecost* (Greek word meaning "50"), which is the next festival.

On the 33rd day of the "Counting of the Omer," there is a minor holiday. The Talmud records that it was the day a cruel plague ended.

In the first century, the highly revered Rabbi Akiva's 24,000 disciples died during this period of time. The Talmud teaches they were guilty of a lack of unity and not treating one another with respect. On the 33rd day of the Counting of the Omer, a holiday is celebrated commemorating the date the plague stopped. In Israel, on this date, campfires are built and people roast potatoes and sing songs.

Historically on Aviv 17, the date of the Festival of Firstfruits, the Children of Israel crossed the Red Sea after leaving Egypt. The Egyptian army went into the Red Sea to attack the Children of Israel, but God caused the waters to drown the army and the Pharaoh. Therefore, the Children of Israel emerged alive on the 17th, the same date as Yeshua's resurrection.

In order for the Children of Israel to go to the Promised Land, they had to be set free from the Pharaoh's ownership. With his death in the Sea, they were free to go.

Before the Children of Israel crossed the Red Sea, they secured the remains of Joseph on Aviv 15. **(Exodus 13:19-20)** An interesting parallel is that Yeshua had been placed in the tomb of Joseph of Arimathea on Aviv 15. **(Matthew 27:59-60)**

In **Hebrews 11**, it states that Joseph **by faith** had given the commandment that they take his bones when they left Egypt.

And Joseph said to his brethren, "I am dying; but God will surely visit you, and bring you out of this land to the land of which He swore to Abraham, to Isaac, and to Jacob." Then Joseph took an oath from the Children of Israel, saying, "God will surely visit you, and you shall carry up my bones from here." (Genesis 50:24-25)

Why did Joseph ask them to take his bones with them?

I think he was looking ahead to the resurrection. I believe he longed to be a part of that which was yet to come and he made provision to have his bones taken to the Promised Land because he saw what would take place in the future.

Following Yeshua's resurrection, the graves of many of the saints were opened and they went into the city and appeared to many people. What became of them is a *mystery.*

When, behold, the veil of the temple was torn in two from top to bottom; and the earth quaked, and the rocks were split, and the graves were opened; and many bodies of the saints who had fallen asleep were raised; and coming out of the graves after His resurrection, they went into the holy city and appeared to many. (Matthew 27:51-53)

I wonder if Joseph was among these that were resurrected, along with Abraham, Isaac and Jacob?

Abraham had secured his burial place in a cave a few miles south of Jerusalem before his death. According to **Genesis 49:29-31**, Abraham's cave at Machpelah was where Abraham and Sarah were buried, along with Isaac, Rebekah, Jacob and Leah.

I believe that this story about the bones of Joseph gives us great hope in the resurrection that is to come!

After retrieving the bones of Joseph and crossing the Red Sea, the Children of Israel traveled 47 days until they reached Mt. Sinai. They were told to consecrate themselves for three days because on the 50th day, they would receive the Torah. The giving of the Torah on Mt. Sinai occurred on the same date as *Shavuot* (Pentecost), the next festival.

Our faith is founded upon the foundational truth of the resurrection.

And if Yeshua is not risen, your faith is futile; you are still in your sins! (1 Corinthians 15:17)

We must believe in our hearts that Yeshua has risen from the dead in order to obtain salvation.

If you confess with your mouth Yeshua, and believe in your heart that God has raised Him from the dead, you will be saved. (Romans 10:9)

Yeshua's resurrection is the promise of the future resurrection of believers.

For the hour is coming in which all who are in the graves will hear His voice and come forth—those who have done good, to the resurrection of life, and those who have done evil, to the resurrection of condemnation. (John 5:28-29)

Events that occurred on the Festival of Firstfruits (Aviv 17):

- Noah's ark rests on Mount Ararat **(Genesis 8:4)**
- Children of Israel cross the Red Sea and the Pharaoh dies in the Sea. **(Exodus 3:18; 5:3;14:25-31)**
- Children of Israel eat the firstfruits of the Promised Land. The manna ceased on the 16th day of Aviv. The day following, Aviv 17, they ate the firstfruits of the Promised Land. **(Joshua 5:10-12)**
- Haman is defeated and hung. In the book of Esther, Haman plots to kill the Jews. He is a type of the *false messiah* (antichrist). On Aviv 13, a decree is issued for all Jews to be killed. **(Esther 3:12)** Esther calls a three day fast, which would be Aviv 14-16. **(Esther 4:16)** On the 16th of Aviv, she risks her life to get an appointment with the

king. She invites him to a banquet. At the banquet, the king asks her what she wants and she invites him to come to another banquet the next day, the 17th of Aviv. On this day, Haman, is hung.

- The resurrection of Yeshua. **(John 12:24, 1 Corinthians 15:16-20)**

Chapter 11

SHAVUOT (PENTECOST)

תֵּשַׁהֹס

The Lord told the Children of Israel when they arrived in the Promised Land and had their first harvest, to count from the day of the waving of the sheaf of firstfruits 49 days, or seven Sabbaths. Then they were to count the day following, which was the 50th day to celebrate the Festival of Shavuot, also known as "Pentecost." It was one of the three festivals that all Jewish males were required to go to in Jerusalem. **(Deuteronomy 16:16)**

From the day after the Sabbath, the day you brought the sheaf of the wave offering, count off seven full weeks. Count off fifty days up to the day after the seventh Sabbath, and then present an offering of new grain to the Lord. (Leviticus 23:15-16)

In Greek, *Pentecost* means "50," which can represent liberty, freedom, or deliverance. Every 50th year in Israel was called the "Year of Jubilee." Slaves were set free and debts were cancelled. Liberty was proclaimed throughout the land by the sound of the Jubilee trumpets. **(Leviticus 25:8-17)** Priests served until the age of 50, then they were at liberty to retire from doing that service. **(Numbers 8:23-26)**

After Yeshua's resurrection, He appeared to His disciples for 40 days, speaking to them of the things pertaining to the Kingdom of God. After 40 days, He ascended back to the Father.

Ten days later (fifty days after the resurrection), the disciples were together in the upper room when the **"Day of Pentecost"** was fully come. **(Acts 2:1)**

The Holy Spirit came like a mighty rushing wind and there appeared tongues of fire. They all spoke in other tongues. **(Acts 2:2-4)**

This happened on the **same date** as the **Giving of the Law** on Mt. Sinai 1,500 years prior. After leaving Egypt on Passover, the Children of Israel went through the Red Sea on Firstfruits, and then traveled 47 days to Mt. Sinai where God told them to consecrate them-selves because He would speak to them in three days, which was the same date as *Shavuot* (Pentecost).

The entire people (estimated at two to three mil-lion) heard God speak on that mountain. He didn't just appear to Moses in private. It was a national revelation! It is written that the whole world heard. According to Jewish tradition, God spoke not only in Hebrew, but also in every known tongue at that time.

In the **Authorized Prayer Book**, Rabbi Hertz, states on page 791:

The Revelation at Sinai, it was taught, was given in desert territory, which belongs to no one nation exclu-sively; and it was heard not by Israel alone, but by the inhabitants of all the earth. The Divine voice divided itself into the 70 tongues then spoken on earth, so that all the children of men might understand its world-embracing and man-redeeming message.

What a *mystery!*

The people actually saw the sound waves that came from the Almighty's mouth and they visualized them as a fiery substance!

In the book **The Midrash Says on Shemot,** by Rabbi Moshe Weissman, on page 182, it says:

On the occasion of matan Torah (the giving of the Torah), the Bnai Yisrael (the children of Israel) not only heard Hashem's (the Lord's) Voice but actually saw the sound waves as they emerged from the Hashem's (the Lord's) mouth. They visualized them as a fiery substance. Each commandment that left Hashem's (the Lord's) mouth traveled around the entire Camp and then to each Jew individually, asking him, "Do you accept upon yourself this Commandment with all the halachot (Jewish law) pertaining to it?" Every Jew answered "Yes" after each commandment. Finally, the fiery substance, which they saw, engraved itself on the luchot (tablets).

In Exodus we read:

Then it came to pass on the third day, in the morning, that there were thunderings and lightnings, and a thick cloud on the mountain; and the sound of the trumpet was very loud, so that all the people who were in the camp trembled. And Moses brought the people out of the camp to meet with God, and they stood at the foot of the mountain. Now Mount Sinai was completely in smoke, because the Lord descended upon it in fire. Its smoke ascended like the smoke of a furnace, and the whole mountain quaked greatly. And when the blast of the trumpet sounded

long and became louder and louder, Moses spoke, and God answered him by voice. (Exodus 19:16-19)

Now all the people witnessed the thunderings, the lightning flashes, the sound of the trumpet, and the mountain smoking; and when the people saw it, they trembled and stood afar off. Then they said to Moses, "You speak with us, and we will hear; but let not God speak with us, lest we die. (Exodus 20:18-19)

After God spoke the Ten Commandments and everyone heard them, Moses went up on the mountain and was taught the rest of the Oral Law which he transmitted to the nation. He was given 613 commandments, along with a detailed explanation on how to fulfill them.

Here, at Mount Sinai, God established the Aaronic priesthood, the sacrificial system, the Tabernacle, and the festivals. Forty years later, just prior to his death, Moses wrote the instructions in the written Torah and gave it to the Jewish people.

Much of the instructions on how to celebrate the festivals were contained in the Oral Law. The Oral Law was incorporated into the Mishnah in the second century, which became the cornerstone of the Gemara,[17] which consists of discussions and debates by the Hebrew sages. The Mishnah and the Gemara together make up the Talmud.

The Talmud says that they actually stood under the mountain at the giving of the Law. (Talmud, Shabos 88a)

R'avdimi bar Chama bar Chasa said, *This teaches us that the Holy One, blessed is He, covered them with the mountain as though it were an upturned vat and He said to them: "If you accept the Torah, well and good. But if not, your burial will be right here!"*

We see many parallels to what happened on Mt. Sinai and what happened in **Acts 2** on the exact same date 1,500 years later!

At both occasions, on Sinai and in Jerusalem, there were similar supernatural manifestations: a mighty rushing wind, tongues of fire, and everyone heard the message in their own language.

After the Giving of the Law, the Bible states that 3,000 of the Children of Israel were slain for their sin of worshipping the golden calf. **(Exodus 32:28)** After Pentecost in **Acts 2,** Peter preaches the gospel and 3,000 were saved. **(Acts 2:38-41)**

He has made us competent as ministers of a new covenant–not of the letter, but of the Spirit; for THE LETTER KILLS, but the SPIRIT GIVES LIFE. (2 Corinthians 3:6)

The Lord declares that He will make a **New Covenant** with the House of Israel and He will put the law in their minds and write it on their hearts. **(Jeremiah 31:31-33)**

The ministry that Yeshua received is superior to the old as it is founded on better promises. We are told in **Hebrews 8:6-13,** that the first covenant has now been made **obsolete**. The dictionary definition of **obsolete** is "no longer in use."

In Galatians 4, the Apostle Paul likens the two covenants to Abraham's two sons, Ishmael and Isaac. Ishmael was born by the slave woman, Hagar, and is likened to Mount Sinai and the Old Covenant. Isaac was born by the free woman, Sarah, and is likened to the New Jerusalem and the New Covenant.

What is absolutely amazing is that Isaac, the child of promise and representative of the New Covenant, was born at *the "**set time**"* on the ***same date*** that both covenants were given! (**Genesis 17:21**; The Book of Jubilees 16:13[18])

Did you know that, according to Jewish tradition, King David was born and died on Shavuot (Pentecost)?

Another *mystery*!

This festival takes place during the wheat harvest. The Book of Ruth is read at this festival. Ruth, a Moabite, was King David's great-grandmother and was a Gentile who converted to Judaism. She is in the lineage of the Messiah!

In ancient Israel, at Shavuot (Pentecost), two huge leavened loaves were waved before the Lord. Many believers think the loaves represent Jew and Gentile brought together as one loaf.

Kevin Connor writes in **The Feasts of Israel**: *In the making of the two Pentecostal wave loaves, many grains*

of wheat, crushed into fine flour, baked in the oven, were united together. All symbolized the union of the Jew and Gentile as the bread of God, for we being many are one body and one bread. **(1 Corinthians 10:16-17)**

For He Himself is our peace, who has made both one, and has broken down the middle wall of separation, having abolished in His flesh the enmity, that is, the law of commandments contained in ordinances, so as to create in Himself ONE NEW MAN from the two, thus making peace, and that He might reconcile them both to God in one body through the cross, thereby putting to death the enmity. (Ephesians 2:14-16)

Today this festival is observed on the 6th of *Sivan* on the Hebraic calendar (May or June on the Gregorian calendar). The synagogue is decorated with greens and flowers because, according to tradition, the surrounding desert bloomed when God spoke at Mt. Sinai. Jews go to the synagogue to hear the reading of The Ten Commandments. The Book of Ruth is also read publicly.

Women light special candles to usher in the holiday. It is customary to stay up all night learning Torah (to atone for those who fell asleep at Sinai). Today, dairy foods are eaten, including ice cream, cheese blintzes, and cheesecake. What a great tradition!

There are different reasons given for eating dairy foods on this festival:

- The numerical value for the Hebrew word for milk is 40 and it commemorates the 40 days that Moses spent on Sinai receiving the entire Torah.
- The Promised Land was referred to as the land flowing with "milk and honey."

Yeshua's time on earth, in joining with the human race, had at its core the fulfillment of the *moedin* (appointments). His **death** on *Passover*, His **burial** on the *Festival of Unleavened Bread*, His **resurrection** on *Firstfruits*, and the **outpouring of the Holy Spirit** on *Shavuot* (Pentecost), fulfilled the Spring festivals that were instituted from heaven.

According to the Bible and Jewish tradition, other events that occurred on Shavuot (Pentecost):
- Abraham died. (The Book of Jubilees 22:1)
- Judah, one of Jacob's sons, was born. (The Book of Jubilees 28:15)
- Isaac was born. (The Book of Jubilees 16:13)
- King David was born and died on this date. (Jewish History, www.chabad.org)
- Jacob and Laban bound themselves by mutual vows. (The Book of Jubilees 29:7)
- Enoch was born and taken to heaven on *Shavuot* (Pentecost). (Chuck Missler, Koinonia House, http://www.khouse.org/articles/1994/101/)
- The infant Moses was rescued from the Nile River. (**Artscroll Mesorah Publications on Shavuot**. ArtScroll is commentaries from an Orthodox Jewish perspective published by Mesorah Publications, Ltd., based in New York.)
- Issachar, one of Jacob's 12 sons, was conceived. (**Genesis 30:14** and **Encyclopedia of Creation Science**)
- Tribe of Benjamin got wives. (**Judges 21:15-24**)
- King Saul was anointed. (**1 Samuel 10:1-7**)

- King Asa and the people of Judah entered into a covenant to seek God. **(1 Chronicles 15)**
- Messiah's Sermon on the Mount. (**Luke 6:12-49,** *"In those days"* refers to *"the Counting of the Omer."*)

Just as the Spring festivals taught on Yeshua's First Coming, we'll now explore the Fall festivals that teach on Yeshua's Second Coming.

Chapter 12

ROSH HASHANA (FEAST OF TRUMPETS)

אנאהסאה הסֹף

Rosh Hashanah, also known as the "Feast of Trumpets," literally means "head of the year." According to Jewish tradition, it marks the anniversary of the creation of Adam and Eve. This festival occurs on the first and second days of the Hebrew month of Tishri (September or October on the Gregorian calendar).

Speak to the children of Israel, saying: In the seventh month, on the first day of the month, you shall have a Sabbath-rest, a memorial of blowing of trumpets, a holy convocation. (Leviticus 23:24)

Tishri is the first month on the civil calendar and the seventh month on the religious calendar. Some rabbinical commentaries state that Adam and Eve were created on this day and also sinned on this day. (Talmud, Sanhedrin 38b; and Midrash[19] Vayikra Rabba 29:1)

Today, the custom on Rosh Hashanah is to **hear** the sounding of the shofar. It's also customary to dip apples in honey and wish each other a sweet new year.

It's interesting that the Mishnah teaches that Jacob was born on Rosh Hashanah. Isaac blessed Jacob with the words: ***"The fragrance of my son is like the fragrance of a field which God has blessed." (Genesis 27:27)*** The Talmud identifies this field as an apple orchard. *(Ta'anis 29b, Biyur Hagra)*

A festive meal is shared to celebrate the new year and a special round loaf of challah bread, which is symbolic of the cycle of time, is generally served. Work is prohibited and religious Jews spend much of the holiday attending synagogue.

Some Jews practice a custom known as *tashlich* ("casting off" sin) in which they throw pieces of bread into a flowing body of water while confessing and repenting of sin and reciting prayers. The bread symbolizes the sins of the past year.

These verses from the book of Micah are recited as they cast their bread into the water. (According to the Mishnah, both Abraham and Jacob were born at this festival and their names are referenced in these verses.)

Who is a God like you, who pardons sin and forgives the transgression of the remnant of his inheritance? You do not stay angry forever but delight to show mercy. You will again have compassion on us; you will tread our sins underfoot and hurl all our iniquities into the depths of the sea. You will be faithful to JACOB, and show love to ABRAHAM, as you pledged on oath to our ancestors in days long ago. (Micah 7:18-20)

On the first of Tishri, a *shofar* (an instrument made from a curved ram's horn) is blown. It is distinctive from the silver trumpets blown on other new moons. The priest chosen to blow the shofar on Rosh Hashana was trained for his calling since his youth. He was an artist, a virtuoso of sacred song. The shofar had to be in perfect condition as the Mishnah forbade the use of any shofar that was not perfect.

According to Saadia Gaon, a ninth century Jewish scholar, who wrote **<u>Ten Reasons for the Shofar to be Blown on Rosh Hashanah</u>**, the ninth reason had to do with the resurrection of the dead. The ancient Jewish understanding was that this would occur at the time known as the **last trump**. According to Jewish scholars, one of the names for the Festival of Rosh Hashanah is the **last trump**.

Behold, I tell you a MYSTERY: We shall not all sleep, but we shall all be changed—in a moment, in the twinkling of an eye, at the LAST TRUMP. For the trumpet will sound, and the dead will be raised incorruptible, and we shall be changed. (1 Corinthians 15:51-52)

The Midrash teaches us that Rosh Hashanah was the day that Abraham went to sacrifice his son, Isaac. The *shofar* (ram's horn) serves as a reminder of God's provision of a ram as a substitute. The Scriptural reading of the binding of Isaac is read on the first day of Rosh

Hashanah in Reform[20] synagogues, but on the second day in Orthodox synagogues.

Abraham believed that God could raise his son from the dead. Hope in the resurrection was a part of Abraham's faith.

By faith Abraham, when he was tested, offered up Isaac, and he who had received the promises offered up his only begotten son, of whom it was said, "In Isaac your seed shall be called," concluding that God was able to raise him up, even from the dead, from which he also received him in a figurative sense. (Hebrews 11:17-19)

The rabbis teach that Isaac was 37 years old at the time of the sacrifice. (Midrash, Genesis Rabbah 56:8)[21] Isaac was a type of Yeshua. He carried his own wood to Mount Moriah, even as Yeshua carried his own cross.

It's significant that the binding of Isaac took place on Mount Moriah because it would become the future site of Solomon's Temple, where sacrifices would be made. It was the same location of the threshing floor that King David purchased from Ornan to build an altar. **(2 Chronicles 3:1)**. Ornan had tried to give the threshing floor to him, but King David insisted on paying for it.

I insist on paying you for it. I will not sacrifice to the Lord my God burnt offerings that cost me nothing. (2 Samuel 24:24)

Teshuvah

Teshuvah, which means to "repent" or "return," is a 40-day period that begins on the first day of the month of *Elul* (August or September on the Gregorian calendar) and ends on *Yom Kippur* (Day of Atonement).

Elul is an acronym for *"I am my Beloved's and my Beloved is mine."* **(Song of Songs 6:3)**

According to the Rabbis, man is born with an evil inclination to sin, of which repentance is the antidote. Repentance can be defined as "to **return** to God."

Come, let us RETURN to the Lord. He has torn us to pieces but He will heal us; He has injured us but He will bind up our wounds. After TWO DAYS He will revive us; on the THIRD DAY He will restore us, that we may live in His presence. Let us acknowledge the Lord; let us press on to acknowledge Him. As surely as the sun rises, He will appear; He will come to us like the WINTER RAINS, like the SPRING RAINS that water the earth. (Hosea 6:1-3)

In Judaism, there is a distinction made between repentance for sins committed against God and those sins committed against our fellow man. If a person sins against another person, he must make restitution with that person before coming to God.

Therefore if you bring your gift to the altar, and there remember that your brother has something against you; leave your gift at the altar and go thy way; first be reconciled to your brother, and then come and offer your gift. (Matthew 5:23-24)

The season of **Teshuvah** is a time for each man to examine his life. It's a time to restore relationships. When we understand that Rosh Hashanah is The Day of Judgment, and the heavenly court reviews each person this day, repentance becomes an important issue.

A future Rosh Hashanah will begin *The Day of the Lord* (which includes the *birth pains*, also known as the "tribulation period.") This concept was taught in the previous chapter entitled **The Day of the Lord** and will be developed in the future section on the **birth pains**.

In **Zephaniah 2,** we read about being gathered together and hidden before **the day of the Lord's anger** *if* we repent.

Gather yourselves together, O shameful nation, before the APPOINTED TIME arrives and THAT DAY sweeps on like chaff, before the fierce anger of the Lord comes upon you, before THE DAY OF THE LORD'S WRATH comes upon you. Seek the Lord, all you humble of the land, you who do what He commands. Seek righteousness, seek humility; perhaps you will be sheltered on THE DAY OF THE LORD'S ANGER. (Zephaniah 2:1-3)

Beginning on the first day of Elul and continuing throughout the entire month, the shofar was blown in ancient Israel to call the nation to repentance and to return to God. It's a yearly **wake-up call** that reminds people of the approach of Judgment Day, which is Rosh Hashanah.

One of the themes of Rosh Hashanah is to **awaken from slumber.** It is thought that the Apostle Paul wrote the book of Ephesians during this season.

Wake up, sleeper, rise from the dead, and Christ will shine on you. (Ephesians 5:14)

In many Jewish communities, **Psalms 27** is recited twice a day during the season of Teshuvah. This passage indicates that the righteous will be hidden during the *time of trouble*, which is the "tribulation period."

For in the TIME OF TROUBLE (Jacob's trouble), He shall hide me in His pavilion: in the secret of His tabernacle shall He hide me; He shall set me high upon a rock. (Psalms 27:5)

It is customary, when writing a letter during Elul, to include wishes for the recipient's well being in the next year and for receiving a good judgment on Rosh Hashanah.

Resurrection of the Dead

According to the Talmud, Rosh Hashana 16b, the resurrection of the dead will occur on **Yom haDin** (The Day of Judgment), which is another name for Rosh Hashanah.

On the six thousandth Rosh Hashana, the shofar will sound and there will be a resurrection of the righteous dead as well as *the **catching away*** of the righteous that are alive at that time. We commonly call this the *"rapture."*

I've heard Bible teachers say that there is no mention of the word **rapture** in the Bible. In reality, we get the term from the following verse:

Then we who are alive and remain shall be CAUGHT UP together with them in the clouds to meet the Lord in the air. (1 Thessalonians 4:17)

The Greek word for "caught up" is *harpuzo*. This word, when translated into Latin, is *raptiere*. When *raptiere* was translated into English, the word *"rapture"* was coined.

The Greek word *harpuzo* means "to catch away." Its Hebrew equivalent is *natzal* and it means "to pluck away" or "a radical departure."

In **2 Thessalonians**, Paul wrote to the Church in Thessalonica that **the coming of the Lord** must be preceded by the *apostasia* first. The word *apostasia* was translated as "falling away," causing some to believe that there will be a great apostasy, or falling away from the faith, at the end of the age. Kenneth Wuest, a noted Greek scholar, states that this is a mistranslation of the Greek word *apostasia*, and a better translation would be "departure."

Liddell and Scott in their classical Lexicon give a second meaning of *apostasia* as "a departure, a disappearance." According to that translation, judgment will occur after the departure or disappearance of the righteous, not a great "falling away" from the faith.

Let no one deceive you by any means; for that Day will not come unless the FALLING AWAY (DEPARTURE, DISAPPEARANCE) comes first, and the man of sin is revealed (the False Messiah), the son of perdition. (2 Thessalonians 2:3)

At Rosh Hashanah, the righteous, both living and dead, from Adam to present, will receive their glorified bodies and will be gathered together for the Coronation of the King and the Wedding of the Messiah, during the time of judgment on earth.

Bridegroom, King, and Judge

Yeshua emphasized the revelation of God as a **Bridegroom, King,** and **Judge** in His final public message to Israel **(Matthew 22:1-14)** and in His final message to the apostles before his crucifixion. **(Matthew 25)**

Isaiah 61-63 reveals the Messianic Redeemer as **Bridegroom, King,** and **Judge.**

The final revelation in the Scriptures reveals Yeshua as **Bridegroom, King** and **Judge. (Revelation 19-22)**

The major themes of Rosh Hashanah (Feast of Trumpets) are the **Wedding** of **the Messiah,** the **Coronation of the King,** and **Judgment.**

Judgment

Rosh Hashanah is known as *Yom HaDin*, the "Day of Judgment." Tradition has it that this is the day we are judged by God.

The blowing of the shofar is an awakening call for people to return and repent. Rabbi Irving Greenberg, in **The Jewish Way, Living the Holidays,** New York, 1988, p. 195, states: *"In the trial imagery, the shofar blast communicates: Oyez! Oyez! This court is in session! The Right Honorable Judge of the World is presiding!"*

God seems to always warn people before He executes judgment. For example, He warned the people to repent before the Flood and He also warned Nineveh, through the prophet Jonah, to repent before pending destruction.

The blowing of the trumpets was understood to be a call to repent and prepare oneself to stand trial before God who would execute His judgment ten days later on Yom Kippur (Day of Atonement). The book of Jonah is read on Yom Kippur. The repentance of the people of Nineveh serves as an inspiration for us to repent, and shows us that repentance can overturn a Divine decree.

Prior to Rosh Hashanah (Feast of Trumpets), in many Jewish communities, **Ezekiel 33:1-7** is read. This passage has to do with the watchman blowing the trumpet and warning of the judgment to come if there is not repentance.

Three sounds blown by the shofar on this day have by tradition been associated with the three books opened on Rosh Hashanah and sealed on Yom Kippur. The concept of three books comes from **Exodus 32:32-33; Psalm 69:28; Daniel 12: 1; Malachi 3:16; and Revelation 21:27.**

As the Mishnah puts it, *"All [the human beings] are judged on Rosh Hashanah [Yom Teruah], and the [divine] sentence is sealed on Yom Kippur."* (Babylonian Talmud[22], Rosh Hashanah 16a)

These books in heaven remain open for seven days and are closed only at the Great Shofar blast on Yom Kippur (Day of Atonement).

"The central image underlying the days between Rosh Hashana and Yom Kippur is that of a court trial for one's life, which is weighed in the balances." (Moses Maimonides,[23] Mishnah Torah, Laws of Teshuvah 3:4, as cited by Irving Greenberg , p. 119,186)

I watched until thrones were put in place, and the Ancient of Days was seated. The court was seated, and the books were opened. (Daniel 7:9-10)

The Talmud states in Rosh Hashana 16b, version of En Yaakov: *Three books are opened on Rosh Hashanah: one for the* **wholly righteous,** *one for the* **wholly wicked,** *and one for the* **intermediates.** *The wholly righteous are at once inscribed and sealed in the Book of Life; the wholly wicked are at once inscribed and sealed in the Book of Death; and the intermediates are held suspended from Rosh Hashanah until Yom Kippur. If they are found* *worthy, they are inscribed for life; if found unworthy, they are inscribed for death.*

During Teshuvah (the season of repentance prior to Rosh Hashanah), one greets a friend with the greeting, *"May you be inscribed in the Book of Life."* During the ten days between Rosh Hashana and Yom Kippur, known as the Days of Awe, the greeting changes to, *"May you be sealed until the day of redemption."*

The **wholly righteous** are those who have received the righteousness of God by faith in Yeshua. This group includes the Old Testament believers who had faith in the coming Messiah. I believe that the wholly righteous will be hidden during the tribulation period when the wrath of God is being poured out on the earth.

The **wholly wicked** are those who have rejected the Messiah throughout the centuries. Those who are alive at the rapture will face the wrath of God during the tribulation period.

The **intermediates** (average people), both Jew and Gentile, will still have time to turn to God during the tribulation period, as their fate has not yet been decided.

The Day of Jacob's Trouble/The Birth Pains of the Messiah

The ten days from Rosh Hashanah (Feast of Trumpets) to Yom Kippur (Day of Atonement) are called the "High Holy Days" or "Days of Awe." Because Rosh Hashanah is a two-day festival, there are actually seven days between these two festivals. The seven days could be symbolic of the seven years of the birth pains (tribulation period) that will begin on a Rosh Hashanah and end on Yom Kippur seven years later. The term *birth pains of the Messiah* is used throughout rabbinic literature and is also known as *the day of Jacob's trouble.* Christians commonly call this the "tribulation period."

I believe that the birth pains and the rapture will both occur simultaneously on Rosh Hashanah at year 6,000. At the end of the seven years of the birth pains, Yeshua will return to earth with His Bride on Yom Kippur (Day of Atonement) and rule from Jerusalem. (This teaching will be developed in the following chapter on Yom Kippur.)

The Sabbath is a picture of the Messianic Kingdom and, as previously discussed, the seventh day is symbolic of the thousand-year period of time known as the millennium. The priests began each Sabbath by cleansing the altar and the Temple. I believe this is a picture of what will be happening on earth during the time of the birth pains (tribulation period). The Messianic Kingdom will begin with a cleansing, as sin is dealt with among all the nations.

The seven-year period known as the birth pains, or the time of Jacob's trouble, is mentioned throughout the Scriptures. I believe it is the 70th week referred to in the book of Daniel.

Seventy 'sevens' are decreed for your people and your holy city to finish transgression, to put an end to sin, to atone for wickedness, to bring in everlasting righteousness, to seal up vision and prophecy and to anoint the most holy. Know and understand this: from the issuing of the decree to restore and rebuild Jerusalem until the Anointed One, the ruler, comes, there will be seven 'sevens,' and sixty-two 'sevens,' It will be rebuilt with streets and a trench, but in times of trouble. After the sixty-two 'sevens,' the Anointed One will be cut off and will have nothing. The people of the ruler who will come will destroy the city and the sanctuary. The end will come like a flood: War will continue to the end, and desolations have been decreed. He will confirm a covenant with many for one 'seven.' In the middle of the 'seven' he will put an end to sacrifice and offering. And on the wing of the temple he will set up an abomination that causes desolation until the end that is decreed is poured out on him. (Daniel 9:24-27)

There are a variety of views on this passage in Daniel. I agree with the view that the first 69 weeks took place prior to the crucifixion of Yeshua and the final 70th week is still to come.

The starting point of Daniel's 70-weeks prophecy was 445 BCE, when King Artaxerxes permitted Nehemiah to rebuild Jerusalem. (Nehemiah 2) The first seven weeks end around the time of the completion of the rebuilding effort in Jerusalem (approximately 400 BCE). The next 62 weeks end in approximately 30 CE at the time of Yeshua's crucifixion. I believe that the "Church Age" takes place during the gap and the 70th week is symbolic of the **birth pains**, or **the time of Jacob's trouble,** that is to come.

Those who are not resurrected on Rosh Hashanah will experience the tribulation period on earth.

As Jesus was sitting on the Mount of Olives, the disciples came to him privately. "Tell us," they said, "when will this happen, and what will be the sign of your coming and of the end of the age?" Jesus answered: "Watch out that no one deceives you.

For many will come in my name, claiming, 'I am the Messiah,' and will deceive many. You will hear of wars and rumors of wars, but see to it that you are not alarmed. Such things must happen, but the end is still to come. Nation will rise against nation, and kingdom against kingdom. There will be famines and earthquakes in various places. All these are the beginning of BIRTH PAINS. (Matthew 24:3-8)

Daniel refers to the *abomination that causes desolation* in the prophecy of **Daniel 9**. Yeshua also refers to the *abomination that causes desolation* in **Matthew 24**. I believe these passages are referring to the *false messiah,* also known as the "antichrist," who will deceive many.

Many interpret Matthew 24 as being written to the Church, when in actuality I believe it is written to the Jews who have not yet believed in Yeshua. Those who are **in Judea** are told to "flee to the mountains" and are told to *"pray that their flight will not take place on a Sabbath."* This passage is referencing a specific location in Israel and the custom of the Jews to keep the Sabbath.

I believe that the *elect* referenced in **Matthew 24** are Jews, not the Church, as the Apostle Paul refers to the *election* of the Jewish people in the epistle to the Romans and references the *elect* as not yet obtaining salvation.

Therefore I endure all things for the sake of the ELECT, that they also may obtain the salvation which is in Christ Jesus with eternal glory. (2 Timothy 2:10)

The **birth pains** referenced in **Matthew 24** are also known as **the time of Jacob's trouble**. We know that

Jacob is Israel, so it makes sense that God is dealing with the nation of Israel during this time, not the Church.

And He said, "Your name shall no longer be called Jacob, but Israel." (Genesis 32:28)

This will be a horrible time on earth as God is dealing with the nation of Israel and those who have rejected Yeshua as the Messiah.

For thus says the Lord: We have heard a voice of trembling, of fear, and not of peace. Ask now, and see, whether a man is ever in labor with child? So why do I see every man with his hands on his loins like a woman in labor, and all faces turned pale? Alas! For that day is great, so that none is like it; and it is the TIME OF JACOB'S TROUBLE, but he shall be saved out of it. (Jeremiah 30:4-7)

At the end of time, all Israel will be saved, according to this promise in **Romans 11**.

I do not want you to be ignorant of this MYSTERY, brothers, so that you may not be conceited: Israel has experienced a hardening in part until the full number of the Gentiles has come in. And so ALL ISRAEL SHALL BE SAVED. (Romans 11:25-26)

I believe that the following prediction in the Talmud is actually speaking of the seven-year tribulation period on earth that will immediately precede the Second Coming of Yeshua with His Bride (who has been hidden during this time):

"In the week when the son of David comes, in the first year this verse will be fulfilled: 'I will cause it to rain upon one city, and cause it not to rain upon another city.' In the second year the arrows of hunger will be sent forth. In the third a great famine; men, women, and children will

*die; **pious men and saints (will be few),** and the Law will be forgotten by its students. In the fourth, partial plenty. In the fifth, great plenty, when men will eat, drink and be merry, and the Law will return to its students. In the sixth, voices. In the seventh, war; and at the end of the seventh year, the son of David will come." (Talmud, Sanhedrin 97a, Rabbi Simeon Ben Yohai)*

Basically, there will be two things going on during this seven-year period. It's like going to a movie theater where two movies are playing simultaneously in two different rooms. There will be a time of terrible destruction on earth, like a horror movie. The other show takes place in heaven. The Coronation of the King and the Wedding of the Messiah will be taking place–and it will be a beautiful love story!

What side of the theater do you want to be in – do you want to see the horror movie or do you want to experience the love story?

Coronation of the King

A theme associated with Rosh Hashanah is the kingship of God and it's known as **The Day of the Coronation.** From ancient times, Jewish scholars have associated this day with the beginning of the Messianic Kingdom.

God created Adam and Eve on Rosh Hashanah. According to tradition, Adam's first words were, *"The Lord is King forever and ever"* and the echo of his voice rang throughout the world.

In order to have a king, there must be a coronation. In Revelation 4, the Apostle John sees a door standing open in heaven. He is told to *"come up here"* and he immediately sees the **throne of God.** This could be symbolic of the righteous being caught up to heaven on Rosh Hashanah.

There are four parts to an enthronement of a Jewish king:

1. A rod or scepter is given.

    He Himself (Messiah) will rule them with a <u>rod of iron</u>. He Himself treads the winepress of the fierceness and wrath of Almighty God. (Revelation 19:15)

2. The king ascends to the throne and is anointed as king.

    God has ASCENDED amid shouts of joy, the Lord amid the SOUNDING OF TRUMPETS. Sing praises to God, sing praises; sing praises to our King, sing praises. For God is the King of all the earth; sing to him a psalm of praise! God reigns over the nations; God is seated on his holy throne. (Psalms 47:5-8)

    Psalms 47 is a recurring passage in the Rosh Hashanah liturgy.

3. All the people clap.

    Clap your hands, all you nations; shout to God with cries of joy. For the Lord Most High is awesome, the great KING over all the earth. (Psalms 47:1-2)

4. All of the subjects come to visit the king after he has taken the throne.

    From one New Moon to another and from one Sabbath to another, all mankind will come

and bow down before me," says the Lord.
(Isaiah 66:23)

The apostle Paul writes to the Church in Philippi
that every knee will bow to the name of Yeshua:

That at the name of Yeshua every knee should
bow, of those in heaven, and of those on earth, and of
those under the earth, and that every tongue should
confess that Yeshua is Lord, to the glory of God the
Father. (Philippians 2:10-11)

The Wedding of the Messiah

But you will be called Hephzibah,[24] and your land
Beulah;[25] for the Lord will take delight in you, and
your land will be married. As a young man marries
a young woman, so will your Builder marry you; as
a BRIDEGROOM rejoices over his BRIDE, so will your
God rejoice over you. (Isaiah 62:3-5)

Some of the ancient wedding customs are symbolic
of the Coming of the Heavenly Bridegroom for His Bride.

Many marriages were arranged, but a young man
could propose on his own initiative. He would take a
large sum of money (*bride price*), a betrothal contract,
and a skin of wine and approach the girl's father or
older brothers. The contract was laid out and the bride
price was discussed.

Yeshua came to the home of His bride, earth. He paid
a high price for her.

For you were bought at a price; therefore glorify
God in your body. (1 Corinthians 6:20)

If the father agreed to the contract and the price, the
girl was called in. If she approved, she would drink of

the wine and they would be betrothed. They entered into covenant.

Yeshua entered into a covenant with His bride before His death.

In the same way, after the supper he took the cup saying, "This cup is the new covenant in my blood, which is poured out for you." (Luke 22:20)

Betrothal was legally binding, like a marriage. A *ketubah* (marriage contract) was drawn up that contained the promises of the groom and the rights of the bride. The Bible is our ketubah.

A typical betrothal period was one to two years. They were usually not allowed to see each other during that time.

You have heard Me say to you, 'I am going away and coming back to you.' (John 14:28)

The bride would immerse herself in a *mikvah*, which is a "ritual cleansing bath," indicating a separation from a former way of life to a new way of life, on the morning of her wedding day.

John the Baptist, the son of a Priest, was known as the **Immerser** and the **Friend of the Bridegroom**. Baptism was the equivalent to immersing in the mikvah.

The bridegroom would leave the girl and go to his father's house to prepare a place for her. He would then begin to work on the *chadar* (wedding chamber). The wedding chamber had to be a beautiful place to bring his bride.

Yeshua was using wedding language when he said:

In My Father's house are many mansions; if it were not so, I would have told you. I go to prepare a place for you. And if I go and prepare a place for

you, I will come again and receive you to Myself; that where I am, there you may be also. (John 14:2-3)

The young man could only come and get the bride when his father said it was time. He would not know when his father would declare that the chamber was ready and send him to get her.

Yeshua was using wedding language when He said:

But of that day and hour no one knows, not even the angels in heaven, nor the Son, but only the Father. (Mark 13:32)

The bride would not know the exact hour of her bridegroom's return. She would have to be prepared and ready. Typically, the bridegroom came in the middle of the night to steal her away.

Yeshua will also come like a *thief in the night.*

For you yourselves know perfectly that the day of the Lord so comes as A THIEF IN THE NIGHT. (1 Thessalonians 5:2)

The bridegroom would be dressed like a king. He would call his close friends together and leave his father's house and begin a procession to the house of the bride. Bystanders would begin to shout, *"Behold the Bridegroom cometh!"* Others would join in until the **shout** could be heard outside the bride's house.

For the Lord Himself will descend from heaven with a SHOUT, with the voice of an archangel, and with the trumpet of God. (1 Thessalonians 4:16-17)

She had very little time to get ready. Her friends would help her get dressed. She dressed as a queen with jewels and her hair was often braided with gold and jewels. She would have a veil over her face.

Let us rejoice and be glad and give Him glory! For the wedding of the Lamb has come, and His Bride has made herself ready. (Revelation 19:7)

Following the ceremony, they would go into a special bridal chamber where the groom would give gifts to the bride.

We read in Isaiah 26, that the bride will be sheltered in the wedding chamber during the time of trouble on earth.

Rosh Hashanah is also known as *Yom HaKeseh* (Day of Concealment), because it is the only festival that falls on the first day of the month and its advent awaits the appearance of the new moon, so the hour and the day of its arrival is not known in advance. It is a two-day period that is also referred to as **the day that nobody knows.**

Yeshua said, "But of that day and hour knows no man, no, not the angels of heaven, but my Father only" "Therefore keep watch, because you do not know on what day your Lord will come." (Matthew 24:36, 42).

The following passage contains language that would identify it with being Rosh Hashanah. It lets us know that the bride will be sheltered during the tribulation period and the rapture will occur on this festival.

Isaiah 26:2, 9, 17, 19-21

2 OPEN THE GATES that the righteous nation may enter, the nation that keeps faith.

In Judaism, the concept of the gates of heaven opening is associated with the Musaf [26] service of Rosh Hashanah.

9 When your JUDGMENTS come upon the earth, the people of the world learn righteousness.

Rosh Hashanah is known as *The Day of Judgment.*

17 As a pregnant woman about to give BIRTH writhes and cries out in her PAIN, so were we in your presence, Lord

The *birth pains* (tribulation period) will begin on Rosh Hashanah.

19 But your dead will live, Lord; their bodies will RISE— let those who dwell in the dust WAKE UP and shout for joy— your dew is like the dew of the morning; the earth will give birth to her dead.

Rosh Hashanah is also known as *Yom Teruah*, the **"Day of the Awakening Blast."** It is taught in the Talmud that the resurrection of the dead will occur on Rosh Hashanah.

20 Go, my people, enter your rooms and shut the doors behind you; HIDE YOURSELVES for a little while until HIS WRATH has passed by.

We are not appointed to *wrath,* also known as the "tribulation period." **(1 Thessalonians 1:10, 5:9, Revelation 3:10)**

21 See, the Lord is coming out of his dwelling to punish the people of the earth for their sins.

I believe that those who are being punished are those who are alive and have rejected Yeshua as the Messiah. The righteous are hidden in the wedding chamber during this time.

In the ancient wedding ceremony, the bride and the bridegroom would go to the bridal chamber for a week. The friend of the bridegroom would stand by the door of the chamber and signal the guests when the marriage had been consummated. After his announcement, a seven-day period of festivities would begin. During the seven days, the bride remains hidden in the bridal chamber.

Genesis 29:27 mentions the custom of the **bridal week.** The bridal week corresponds to the seven years when the Bride will be hidden during the time of wrath on earth. The word "week" in Hebrew is *shavuah.* It means "a seven." It can mean **seven days** or **seven years**. (An example of this Hebrew word *shavuah* meaning "seven" years can be found in **Daniel 9:27**.)

After the bridegroom and bride emerge from the wedding chamber after seven days, the actual wedding feast takes place. (This subject will be addressed in the chapter on *Sukkot,* known as "The Feast of Tabernacles.")

Yeshua began his public ministry at a wedding. **(John 2)** He ended his ministry declaring that the Kingdom of God was like a wedding. **(Matthew 22:1-14)**

Throughout the Bible, we see Yeshua presented as the Bridegroom God. Yeshua's ministry was introduced by John the Baptist, functioning as the Friend of the Bridegroom, **(John 3:29)**, and it ended with the Apostle John revealing the Bride **(Revelation 19-22).**

The *mystery* that Yeshua will return for His Bride on the festival of Rosh Hashanah is being unsealed through understanding festival language and the ancient wedding customs.

For this reason a man shall leave his father and mother and be joined to his wife, and the two shall become one flesh. This is a great MYSTERY, but I speak concerning Christ and the church. (Ephesians 5:31-32)

With great anticipation, the Spirit and the Bride say, *"Come!"* **(Revelation 22:17)**

According to Rabbinic tradition, (Rabbi Eliezer, Mishnah Tractate on Rosh Hashanah 10b-11a), the following occurred on a Rosh Hashanah:

- Abraham was born.
- Jacob was born.
- Joseph was freed from prison.
- It was decreed on Rosh Hashanah that Sarah, Rachel, and Hannah would conceive their sons Isaac, Joseph, and Samuel. All had been barren prior to the decrees.

Chapter 13

YOM KIPPUR (DAY OF ATONEMENT)

רְפִפְכ מִי

Yom *Kippur* is the "Day of Atonement" because *yom* means "day" in Hebrew and *kippur* is from a root word that means, "to atone." It falls on the tenth day of the seventh month in Tishri (September or October on the Gregorian calendar). It marks the culmination of the *Days of Awe* that follow Rosh Hashana (Feast of Trumpets).

The Lord said to Moses, "The tenth day of this seventh month is the DAY OF ATONEMENT. Hold a sacred assembly and deny yourselves." (Leviticus 23:26-27)

Yom Kippur (Day of Atonement) is considered to be the most holy day on the Hebraic calendar. It is the most solemn of all the festivals. According to tradition, God inscribes each person's fate for the coming year in the Book of Life on Rosh Hashana and waits until Yom Kippur to seal the verdict. One of the themes of the Days of Awe is the concept that God has books that He writes our names in, recording who will live and who will die in the next year. The decision is made on Rosh

Hashanah, but our actions during the Days of Awe can change it.

One is encouraged to make amends and ask forgiveness for any sins committed during the past year.

The following is an ancient prayer that has been a part of liturgy of Rosh Hashanah (Feast of Trumpets) and Yom Kippur (Day of Atonement) for centuries:

"On Rosh Hashanah it is written and on Yom Kippur it is sealed: how many will pass away and how many will be created; who will live and who will die, who in due time and who not in due time; who by water and who by fire; who by sword and who by beast; who by tremor and who by plague, but repentance, prayer and righteous giving can avert the ill decree."

The festival of Yom Kippur is observed by a total fast. Abstinence from food and drink, even water, usually begins 20 minutes before sundown and ends after nightfall the following day. It is a day to afflict the soul. There is no eating or drinking, no wearing of comfortable shoes, no bathing or washing, no anointing oneself with perfumes, lotions, or deodorants, and no marital relations. No work is permitted on this day. In Israel today, everything is shut down – no radio or television or public transportation.

It is customary to wear white. This reminds me of **Isaiah 1:18** that promises that our sins will be made white as snow. Most of the day is spent in the synagogue in prayer and worship. In Orthodox synagogues, services begin early in the morning and continue until about 3:00 pm. There is a short break and the services resume again and end at nightfall.

On this day, one asks God to annul all personal vows that were made the past year that should not have been made. Confession of the sins of the community also takes place led by the leader. For example, all may say together *"Adonai, forgive us for slandering one another this year."* All sins are confessed out loud in the plural, emphasizing corporate responsibility for sin. It's usually a very long list!

The concluding service of Yom Kippur is known as *Ne'ilah,* "the closing of the gates." According to the liturgy of the festivals, the gates of heaven open on Rosh Hashanah and they close on Yom Kippur.

As mentioned in an earlier chapter, I've known people, without any prior knowledge of the festivals, who've had experiences on festival dates. Years ago, a friend told me that she had been awakened on Yom Kippur to the deafening sound of gates slamming shut. It alarmed her and she couldn't understand why she had been allowed to hear that sound. I explained to her that there is coming a day when the gates of heaven will close and it will be too late for anyone to enter in. I believe this experience was motivation to share the good news of the Kingdom with people before it's too late!

The service in the synagogue ends with a long blast of the shofar. Rosh Hashanah (Feast of Trumpets) is known as the *"**last trump**,"* and Yom Kippur (Day of Atonement) is known as the *"**great trump**."*

And in that day a GREAT TRUMP will sound. (Isaiah 27:13)

Yom Kippur recalls the story of when Moses came down from Mt. Sinai after receiving the Ten

Commandments to find Aaron and the Israelites worshipping the golden calf. In his anger, he hurled the tablets to the ground, breaking them. He went back up the mountain on the first day of the month of Elul and sought God's forgiveness for the sin of the Israelites and received a second set of tablets. He returned on Yom Kippur, the 10th of Tishri.

An idiom for Yom Kippur is "**face to face.**" Moses would meet with God and speak to him "**face to face**" as a man speaks to a friend. **(Exodus 33:11)**

It was only on Yom Kippur, the holiest day of the year, that the High Priest could enter the Holy of Holies and utter the name of God because God's name is so holy. *Holy* means "set apart, special; unlike any other."

In ancient times, it was the day of national cleansing. On this day alone, the High Priest entered the Holy of Holies with the blood of a goat, the sin offering. He would sprinkle the blood on the mercy seat.[27] The blood of the sin offering brought about the cleansing of all sin for the nation.

Yeshua made atonement for our sins through the shedding of His blood. He was the sin offering.

He is the atoning sacrifice for our sins, and not only for ours but also for the sins of the whole world. (1 John 2:2)

In order to enter the Holy of Holies, the High Priest would bathe his entire body in a mikvah. When he entered the Holy of Holies, he saw the Lord's presence as a brilliant cloud hovering over the mercy seat.

Many believe that it was on Yom Kippur that John the Baptist baptized Yeshua. There are a few reasons for this belief. Yeshua was our High Priest **(Hebrews 3:1)**, and just as the High Priest would immerse his entire body on Yom Kippur, it makes sense that Yeshua would also be immersed on this day.

Yeshua had just come out of the wilderness after fasting for 40 days and nights before being baptized. This would have been the same time frame that Moses had fasted for 40 days and nights before coming down from the mountain with the second set of tablets on Yom Kippur.

Another reason is that the season of Teshuvah ends on Yom Kippur. It was probably during the season of Teshuvah that John the Baptist began preaching the message of repentance as *teshuvah* means "to repent" or "to return."

In those days John the Baptist came preaching in the wilderness of Judea, saying, "Repent, (Teshuvah) for the kingdom of heaven is at hand!" (Matthew 3:1-2)

The original ceremony for Yom Kippur involved two goats.

He is to take the two goats and present them before the Lord at the entrance to the Tent of Meeting. He is to cast lots for the two goats – one lot for the Lord and the other for the scapegoat. (Leviticus 16:7-8)

As the High Priest killed the first goat, the meaning was clear to the Israelites. They knew it was being killed to cover or atone for their sin. When the blood of the goat was applied to the mercy seat, atonement was made for sin.

The second goat, known as the scapegoat, was taken into the wilderness and pushed over a cliff after the high priest laid the sins of the people on its head. It was a custom to tie a red sash on this goat and a red sash on the door of the Temple. In connection with this ceremony, the sash on the Temple door would turn white when the goat was pushed off the cliff.

The two goats were considered one offering. Some people believe the scapegoat was a picture of Yeshua who took our sins upon Himself. Others believe that the scapegoat was a type of Satan and that the ceremony of pushing this goat off the cliff is a preview of the angel sending Satan to the abyss.

And I saw an angel coming down out of heaven, having the key to the abyss and holding in his hand a great chain. He seized the dragon, that ancient serpent, which is the devil, or Satan, and bound him for a thousand years. (Revelation 20:1-2)

According to the Talmud (Talmud Bavli, Yoma 19b), something took place 40 years before the destruction of the second Temple in 70 CE. In the year 30 CE, the red sash stopped turning white!

Was it because the crucifixion of Yeshua around that time made the yearly sacrifice of the goats unnecessary?

God presented Messiah as a sacrifice of atonement, through the shedding of his blood—to be received by faith. (Romans 3:25)

We overcome the enemy through the blood of the Lamb.

For the accuser of our brothers and sisters, who accuses them before our God day and night, has been hurled down. They triumphed over him by the blood of the Lamb. (Revelation 12:10-11)

After Yeshua's death on the cross, He ascended to heaven as our High Priest and entered the Holy of Holies once and for all by His own blood.

But when Yeshua came as High Priest of the good things that are now already here, He went through the greater and more perfect tabernacle that is not made with human hands, that is to say, is not a part of this creation. He did not enter by means of the blood of goats and calves; but He entered the Most Holy Place once for all by His own blood, thus obtaining eternal redemption. (Hebrews 9:11-12)

Before He ascended to heaven after His resurrection, Yeshua appeared to Mary Magdalene. He told her not touch Him, as He had not yet ascended to the Father. **(John 20:17)** On Yom Kippur, nobody could touch the High Priest as he ascended to the altar to apply the blood as atonement for sin.

Yeshua is our High Priest and, through his blood, we can now approach God with confidence.

Therefore, since we have a great High Priest who has ascended into heaven, Yeshua the Son of God, let us hold firmly to the faith we profess. Let us then approach God's throne of grace with confidence, so that we may receive mercy and find grace to help us in our time of need. (Hebrews 4:14,16)

After His ascension, eight days later, Yeshua appeared to the apostles and told Thomas to touch his hands and side. **(John 20:26-27)** According to the Law, if you touched a dead body, you would be unclean for seven days. Purification took place on the eighth day.

By slaying animals and applying their blood to the altar, the garments of the High Priest became very bloody. I believe that Yom Kippur (Day of Atonement) is the day Yeshua will return with His Bride at the end of the tribulation period and His garments will be stained red.

Why are your garments red, like those of one treading the winepress? I have trodden the winepress alone; from the nations no one was with me. I trampled them in my anger and trod them down in my wrath; their blood spattered my garments, and I stained all my clothing. (Isaiah 63:2-3)

Yeshua will be dressed in a robe dipped in blood when He returns on Yom Kippur. The armies of heaven will be dressed in white and will be following Him on white horses. Remember, it's customary to dress in white on Yom Kippur.

He is dressed in a robe dipped in blood, and His name is the Word of God. The armies of heaven were following him, riding on white horses and dressed in fine linen, white and clean. Coming out of His mouth is a sharp sword with which to strike down the nations. He will rule them with an iron scepter. He treads the winepress of the fury of the wrath of God Almighty. On His robe and on His thigh He has this name written: King of Kings and Lord of Lords. (Revelation 19:13-16)

At Yeshua's physical return to earth on Yom Kippur, He will destroy all the nations that came against Jerusalem in the Battle of Armageddon. **(Revelation 16:16)**

The word *Armageddon* comes from a Hebrew word that means "Megiddo." The exact location is unclear, but it is believed to be the hill country surrounding the Plain of Megiddo, some 60 miles north of Jerusalem. The *false messiah*, known as the "antichrist," and his followers will be defeated and the Jews will recognize their Messiah.

On that day I will set out to destroy all the nations that attack Jerusalem. And I will pour out on the house of David and the inhabitants of Jerusalem a spirit of grace and supplication. They will look on me, the one they have pierced, and they will mourn for him as one mourns for an only child, and grieve bitterly for him as one grieves for a firstborn son. (Zechariah 12:9-10)

After this final battle, Yeshua will judge and separate the nations. **(Matthew 25:31-34)**

The following verses in Joel 2 contain Yom Kippur language and I believe also substantiates the truth that the Bride will be hidden in the wedding chamber during the tribulation period.

Joel 2

v. 1 Let all who live in the land tremble, for the DAY OF THE LORD is coming. It is close at hand – a day of darkness and gloom, a day of clouds and blackness.

As discussed in an earlier chapter, *The Day of the Lord* refers to the thousand-year millennium and includes the seven-year tribulation period known as the birth pains or the day of Jacob's trouble.

v. 15 Blow the TRUMPET in Zion, declare a holy FAST, call a sacred assembly.

This is clearly Yom Kippur as it is the only festival that requires a **fast.** The trumpet being referred to is the **great trump** that is associated with Yom Kippur.

v. 16 Let the bridegroom leave his room and the bride her chamber.

In the ancient wedding custom, the groom would escort the bride from the bridal chamber at the end of the seven days. I believe the seven days corresponds to the seven years that the Bride will be hidden during the tribulation period on earth.

For now we see only a reflection as in a mirror; then we shall see FACE to FACE. Now I know in part; then I shall know fully, even as I am fully known. (1 Corinthians 13:12)

At the end of the bridal week, the veil would be removed, so that the bride's face could be seen. An idiom associated with Yom Kippur is **"face to face."**

At the end of seven years, on the festival of Yom Kippur (Day of Atonement), the Bride will return with Yeshua to celebrate the wedding feast on earth. *Sukkot,* also known as the "Feast of Tabernacles," is the next festival. I believe it teaches on the wedding feast and the Messianic Kingdom to come.

These events occurred on Yom Kippur:
- Moses came down the mountain with the second set of tablets. **(Exodus 34)**
- Ezekiel was taken and shown the third Temple. **(Ezekiel 40:1)**
- Joseph's brothers sold him into slavery. (Book of Jubilees)
- Jubilee years began on Yom Kippur. **(Leviticus 25:9)**

Chapter 14

SUKKOT (FEAST OF TABERNACLES)

תֻכָּס

The seventh festival is *Sukkot*, commonly known as the "Feast of Tabernacles." It occurs five days after Yom Kippur (Day of Atonement) on the 15th of Tishri (September or October on the Gregorian calendar) and is celebrated for seven days.

Speak unto the children of Israel, saying, 'The fifteenth day of this seventh month shall be the Feast of Tabernacles for seven days unto the Lord.' (Leviticus 23:34)

It's the most joyful of all the festivals and mentioned more times in Scripture than any other. It teaches on the joy of the Messianic Kingdom. Sukkot is so unreservedly joyful that it is commonly referred to in Jewish prayer and literature as the **Season of our Rejoicing.**

The Talmud (Sukkah 5:1a-b) describes one particular ceremony in detail, including how men would dance and do somersaults with flaming torches in their hands while singing songs of praise. The Talmud states, *"He who has not seen the rejoicing at the place of the water-drawing has never seen rejoicing in his life."*

It's a big yearly party! In the time of the Temple, pilgrims came from everywhere. It was a joyous trip with much singing and laughing. They were even told to spend some of their tithe on the festivities, including wine and beer.

You must tithe all of your crops every year. When you arrive, use the money to buy an ox, a sheep, some wine, or beer, to feast there before the Lord your God, and to rejoice with your household. (Deuteronomy 14:22,26, The Living Bible)

The word *sukkot* is the plural of *sukkah*, which refers to the "temporary dwellings" or "huts" that the Jews were commanded to live in during this holiday. Upon arrival in Jerusalem, by Tishri 14, tens of thousands of these structures lined the streets.

And you shall take for yourselves on the first day the fruit of beautiful trees, branches of palm trees, the boughs of leafy trees, and willows of the brook;

and you shall rejoice before the Lord your God for seven days. You shall keep it as a feast to the Lord for seven days in the year. It shall be a statute forever in your generations. You shall celebrate it in the seventh month. You shall dwell in booths for seven days. All who are native Israelites shall dwell in booths. (Leviticus 23:40-42)

I am confident that Yeshua was born at Sukkot (Feast of Tabernacles) in September or October. I believe he was conceived on December 25, which would have been Hanukkah that year. (See Appendix I.)

After learning that Yeshua was born at Sukkot (Feast of Tabernacles) and reading how the date was calculated, I had a conversation with a friend of mine, who is a pastor. He told me that he had figured out that Yeshua was born at this festival mathematically. I was amazed that he had calculated it himself and had come to the same conclusion. He then told me that he had a Masters Degree in mathematics!

The *sukkah* that is built today is a "hut" consisting of temporary walls and an open roof covered by branches or leaves. It serves as a temporary shelter during the festival. Jewish families eat their meals inside it and some even sleep in their sukkah. Most synagogues build a communal sukkah, although most observant families build their own.

Sukkot also commemorates the Jews wandering through the desert for 40 years, during which time they lived in temporary dwellings.

When the Jewish people left Egypt and traveled in the wilderness, they numbered about two to three million people. The wilderness was a place inhabited by deadly snakes and serpents and there was no protection from the burning heat of the sun. According to tradition, God miraculously protected them with seven clouds of glory – four around the side, one above them, one below them like a carpet, and one to lead the way. It was their sukkah. These clouds were later removed when they sinned by worshipping the golden calf. They returned permanently in the month of Tishri when the construction of Moses' tabernacle began, remaining with them for the entire forty years in the wilderness.

Mary and Joseph went to Bethlehem because the Roman census was taking place. **(Luke 2:1-5)** Yeshua was born five miles outside of Jerusalem where the festivities were also taking place. Sukkot was one of the three festivals that Jewish males were required to attend in Jerusalem.

Was Yeshua born in a sukkah?

In Hebrew, a "stable" is called a *sukkah*. **(Genesis 33:17)** Sukkot, the name of this festival, is the plural of this word.

In **John 1:14** it says, *"The Word became flesh and tabernacled among us."* A Jewish translation of that verse reads: *"And Hashem (God) took on gufaniyut (corporeality) and made his SUKKAH, his mishkan (tabernacle) among us."*

This festival is also known as **The Season of our Joy**. An angel declared the message of joy at Yeshua's birth.

But the angel said to them, "Do not be afraid. I bring you good news that will cause great JOY for all the people. Today in the town of David a Savior has been born to you; he is the Messiah, the Lord." (Luke 2:10-11)

It was in context of celebrating the festival of Sukkot that we read the following in the book of Nehemiah:

Then he said to them, "Go your way, eat the fat, drink the sweet, and send portions to those for whom nothing is prepared; for this day is holy to our Lord. Do not sorrow, for the JOY of the Lord is your strength." (Nehemiah 8:10)

Because the festival included the ingathering harvest, it is also known as **The Feast of Ingathering.** Samples of the Fall crops were hung in the sukkah to acknowledge God's faithfulness in providing that year. It is common practice today to decorate the sukkah with fruits and vegetables. Some hang the seven species mentioned in Deuteronomy 8:8 (wheat, barley, vines, figs, pomegranates, olives, and honey) from the roof of their sukkah.

The book of Ecclesiastes is read on Sukkot (Feast of Tabernacles), recalling the impermanence of material things. After the destruction of the first Temple and Exile in 586 BCE, the *sukkot* (temporary dwellings) came to represent the longing for the Messiah and the redemption of the world.

According to tradition, the sukkah commemorates the shelter built by Abraham when he greeted the three messengers (Midrash, Numbers Rabbah 14). This remembrance of Abraham reminds us of his outstanding trait of hospitality. To this day, during this festival, heavenly guests, (Abraham, Isaac, Jacob, Moses, Aaron, Joseph, and King David), are invited to the sukkah each night and places are set for them at the table.

It was on this festival that Yeshua went to the mountain with three of his disciples and was transfigured before them. Peter offered to build *sukkot* (temporary shelters) for Moses and Elijah who appear.

After SIX DAYS Yeshua took with him Peter, James and John the brother of James, and led them up a high mountain by themselves. There He was transfigured before them. His face shone like the sun, and his clothes became as white as the light. Just then there appeared before them Moses and Elijah, talking with Messiah. Peter said to Yeshua, "Lord, it is good for us to be here. If you wish, I will put up three shelters—one for you, one for Moses and one for Elijah." (Matthew 17:1-4)

Why do you think it says that **after six days** Yeshua went up to the mountain? We learned from a previous chapter that these phrases are important. We learned that "a day is as a thousand years" and **six days** is probably a hidden message for the year 6,000. The 1,000-year millennium would be the 7th day and this festival teaches on what will transpire during that time.

I believe it is at this festival that the wedding feast will occur on earth in the Messianic Kingdom, or the Age to Come.

I say to you that many will come from the east and the west, and will take their places at the feast with Abraham, Isaac and Jacob in the kingdom of heaven. (Matthew 8:11)

In the parable of the wedding feast in **Matthew 22:2**, Yeshua said: *"The kingdom of heaven is like a certain king who arranged a marriage for his son."* Not everyone accepted the invitation, however, and some made light of it and even killed some of the king's messengers. It says in verses 7-8: ***"But when the king heard about it, he was furious. And he sent out his armies, destroyed those murderers, and burned up their city."***

Also, when the king discovered that someone was at the wedding feast without a wedding garment, in verse 13, he tells his servants to ***"Bind him hand and foot, take him away, and cast him into outer darkness; there will be weeping and gnashing of teeth."***

I believe this parable corresponds to Sukkot (Feast of Tabernacles) and the judgment that will take place for those who have not put their faith in Yeshua.

In the Talmud, Baba Bathra 74b, it says that Leviathan will be slain and his flesh served as a feast to the righteous in the Age to Come. The Festival of Sukkot concludes with a prayer recited upon leaving the sukkah: *"May it be your will, Lord our God and God of our forefathers, that just as I have fulfilled and dwelt in this sukkah, so may I merit the coming year to dwell in the sukkah of the skin of Leviathan. Next year in Jerusalem."*

During the time of the Temple, a magnificent ceremony took place in which the people rejoiced during the pouring of water and wine over the altar. The High Priest would bring water from the nearby pool of Siloam, known as **living water,** and carry it up to the Temple mount through the huge crowd, in a golden vessel and pour it out over the altar. Next, his assistant would pour wine from a silver vessel over the altar.

This action was repeated every day during the festival. At the same time, priests would cut willow trees at least 25 feet in length and would align themselves shoulder to shoulder in several rows approximately 30 feet apart. They would swing the branches in unison and it would make the sound of a mighty rushing wind as they approached the Temple. They would circle the altar seven times and lay the willows over it, forming a sukkah as the water and wine were being poured out on the altar.

As the living water was drawn from the pool of Siloam, the people sang *Isaiah 12:3: "Therefore with joy shall you draw water out of the wells of salvation."* *(Yeshua* is the same word as "salvation.") It was at this festival, when Yeshua made the mysterious claim that He was the **living water** and that He could meet the deepest need of every human heart.

On the last day, that great day of the feast, Yeshua stood and cried out, saying, "If anyone thirsts, let him come to Me and drink. He who believes in Me, as the Scripture has said, out of his heart will flow rivers of LIVING WATER." (John 7:37-38)

The rabbis would teach on every aspect of the festival about a month beforehand, including each reference that dealt with water.

On the last day of this particular festival, the religious leaders brought the woman caught in adultery to Yeshua. He wrote something in the dust (probably their names) and they would have known exactly what He was doing as they would have just taught the following passage:

All who forsake You shall be ashamed. "Those who depart from Me shall be written in the earth, because they have forsaken the Lord, the fountain of living waters." (Jeremiah 17:13)

In the Temple complex during Sukkot, there were four great vats of oil in the Court of Women that illuminated the whole city, and they were known as "the light of the world". It was also at this festival that Yeshua proclaimed that He was **the light of the world.**

Then Yeshua spoke to them again, saying, "I am the LIGHT OF THE WORLD. He who follows Me shall not walk in darkness, but have the light of life." (John 8:12)

During the time of the Temple, 70 animal sacrifices were offered corresponding to the seventy nations of the world. Sukkot is also known as *The Feast of the Nations.* This is reiterated in the Midrash on Psalms 109:4: "*At the Festival of Tabernacles we offer up seventy bullocks (as an atonement) for the seventy nations, and we pray that rain will come down for them.*"

Years ago, a friend of mine, who was not aware that Sukkot was also called The Feast of the Nations, was told by God to buy different cheeses from different countries and to "eat the nations" on this festival date. You can imagine her surprise and delight when she told me about this adventure and I related that another name for Sukkot (Feast of Tabernacles) is **The Feast of the Nations!**

The traditional Bible reading on the second day of Sukkot is taken from **Zechariah 14**. An additional portion is read that speaks of the war of Gog and Magog. **(Ezekiel 38:14-39:16)** The prophet Zechariah spoke of the end of days when Israel would be redeemed and her enemies destroyed. This day of restoration will take place after the "tribulation period" (*the day of Jacob's trouble),* when the Jewish people will cry out to God to deliver them from destruction.

At that time, Israel will be restored and Yeshua will reign from Israel over all the nations of the earth.

The Lord will be King over the whole earth. On that day there will be one Lord, and His name the only name. (Zechariah 14:9)

The nations will celebrate Sukkot (Feast of Tabernacles) in the Messianic Kingdom during the millennium.

And it shall come to pass that everyone who is left of all the nations which came against Jerusalem shall go up from year to year to worship the King, the Lord of hosts, and to keep the Feast of Tabernacles. If any of the peoples of the earth do not go up to Jerusalem to worship the King, the Lord Almighty, they will have no rain. (Zechariah 14:16)

Glory is a major theme of Sukkot. The glory appeared in Solomon's Temple at its dedication on Sukkot (Feast of Tabernacles) and the priests could not stand to minister.

When Solomon finished praying, fire came down from heaven and consumed the burnt offering and the sacrifices, and the glory of the Lord filled the Temple. The priests could not enter the Temple of the Lord because the glory of the Lord filled it. So Solomon observed the festival at that time for seven days. (2 Chronicles 7:1-2, 8)

The *glory* can be defined as a "tangible weighty man-ifestation of God's presence that is discernable to one of our five senses." The glory was manifest in both the tabernacles of Moses and David.

Tabernacle of Moses

When Moses set up the tabernacle in the wilderness, the glory filled it. **(Exodus 40:33-35)** In the glory, all their needs were met. Manna came down from heaven. Even their shoes and clothes did not wear out. They were protected from their enemies and they enjoyed total health. None were weak or sick. A cloud led them during the day and a pillar of fire by night.

Tabernacle of David

David set up a tent for the Ark of the Covenant, with worship continuing around the clock, and God's glory was manifest. David writes in **Psalms 63:2:** *"I have seen you in the sanctuary and beheld your power and your glory!"*

The Tabernacle of David will be restored according to **Amos 9:11** and **Acts 15**.

On THAT DAY I will raise up the tabernacle of David, which has fallen down, and repair its damages; I will raise up its ruins, and rebuild it as in the days of old. (Amos 9:11)

(In the chapter on *The Day of the Lord*, we learned *that day* is a term for the "millennium.")

Sukkot teaches on the Messianic Kingdom to come. The Millennial Kingdom will be established in glory, without the curse of sin. There will be no more war **(Isaiah 2)**, animals will be docile **(Isaiah 11)**, and people will live long lives **(Isaiah 65)**. It will be a time when all the nations will follow the ways of the God of Israel. As a result, *shalom* (peace) and the knowledge of the glory will fill the earth.

For the earth will be filled with the knowledge of the glory of the Lord as the waters cover the sea. (Habakkuk 2:14)

At the end of the thousand years, Satan is loosed and will gather some of the descendants of those who survived the tribulation for one last rebellion. He will be defeated and will be cast into the lake of fire. **(Revelation 20:1-3)**

Judgment will take place at this time. Everyone who was not resurrected with the righteous at the first resurrection (Rosh Hashanah) will experience a bodily resurrection before this final judgment. Some will awaken to life and some to death and condemnation. **(Daniel 12:2 and John 5:28-29)**

The apostle John wrote in **Revelation 20:12: "*And I saw the dead, great and small, standing before the throne.*"**

Anyone whose name was not found written in the Book of Life was thrown into the lake of fire.

Then death and Hades were thrown into the lake of fire. The lake of fire is the second death. Anyone whose name was not found written in the book of life was thrown into the lake of fire. (Revelation 20:14-15)

At that time, those who became believers during the thousand years (the descendants of those who survived the tribulation) now receive their glorified bodies.

An extra day is added to the festival of Sukkot. It is the eighth day, known as *Shemini Atzeret* both in the Bible and in rabbinic literature. Talmudic rabbis treated this day as a separate festival, but today it's mostly regarded as the conclusion of the festival of Sukkot (Feast of Tabernacles).

This eighth day is symbolic of eternity, known as *The World to Come*. This is referenced in the apocryphal Book of Enoch 33:1:[28]

And I appointed the eighth day also, that the eighth day should be the first-created after my work, and that the first seven revolve in the form of the seven thousand, and at the beginning of the eight thousand there should be a time of not-counting, endless, with neither years nor months nor weeks nor days nor hours.

In **Revelation 21**, John describes the nature of the New Heaven and New Earth. He states that the first heaven and earth pass away—without explaining how it actually happens. He then describes the holy city, the New Jerusalem, descending from heaven. There is no Temple because *"its Temple is the Lord God the Almighty and the Lamb." (Revelation 21:22)* There is no more sun or moon because the city is so glorious that it illuminates itself. There is no more night. A new world now replaces the old.

And I heard a loud voice from heaven saying, "Behold, the tabernacle of God is with men, and He will dwell with them, and they shall be His people. God Himself will be with them and be their God. And God will wipe away every tear from their eyes; there shall be no more death, nor sorrow, nor crying. There shall be no more pain, for the former things have passed away." (Revelation 21:3-4)

The culmination of John's vision is like stepping back into the Garden of Eden. Right in the very center of the City, there stands the throne of God and a crystal clear river flows from it. Everything has now come full circle.

They shall see His face, and His name shall be on their foreheads. There shall be no night there: They need no lamp nor light of the sun, for the Lord God gives them light. And they shall reign forever and ever. (Revelation 22:4-5)

Those who have rejected the Lamb (Yeshua) will not be able to enter the New Jerusalem.

Blessed are those who wash their robes, so that they will have the right to the tree of life and may enter the city by the gates. But outside are dogs and sorcerers and sexually immoral and murderers and idolaters, and whoever loves and practices a lie. (Revelation 22:14-15)

The last invitation in the book of Revelation is for anyone who is thirsty to come to the holy city to drink from the water of life.

And the Spirit and the Bride say, "Come!" And let him who hears say, "Come!" And let him who thirsts come. Whoever desires, let him take the water of life freely. (Revelation 22:17)

IN CONCLUSION:
"HOW SHALL WE THEN LIVE?"

Over the years, I've heard some different Bible teachers make these public statements:

"There is nowhere in the Bible that teaches on the pre-tribulation rapture."

"Those that believe in the pre-tribulation rapture are deceived and it's the most dangerous doctrine out there."

"Those that believe in the pre-tribulation rapture are not doing anything except waiting around for Jesus to return."

"Those that believe in the pre-tribulation rapture are stupid."

I do not believe statements like these should be made. They are not true and they are also divisive. I believe that understanding the truths outlined in this book can help bring unity and agreement regarding the controversial subject of the end-times, especially when it comes to the subjects of the rapture and the tribulation period.

In **Titus 2:12-13**, we are told to live soberly, righteously, and godly in this present age, looking for the *Blessed Hope* (the return of Yeshua).

Yeshua told a parable in **Matthew 24** about a servant who wasn't watching for his master's return and began to get drunk and beat other servants. Since he wasn't watching for the return, his master came at a time he wasn't expecting and *"he was assigned a place with the hypocrites where there was weeping and gnashing of teeth."*

We should have a sense of urgency in leading men to repentance. In **2 Peter**, we are told that there will be scoffers in the last days saying, *"Where is the hope of His coming?"* The Apostle Peter explains that Yeshua is not slack in His coming, but is longsuffering as He wants all to come to repentance.

We are to work while it is still day, as night is coming when no man can work. **(John 9:4)**

We are to pray to the Lord of the Harvest to send harvesters out to the harvest field. **(Matthew 9:38)**

We are to forcefully advance the Kingdom of God on earth. **(Matthew 11:12)** The Kingdom of God is advanced whenever someone is saved, delivered, or healed.

In **Luke 19,** we are told to **occupy** until He comes and use our *talents* (the resources and the gifts we have been given) wisely.

We are told to encourage one another with the truth about the rapture. **(1 Thessalonians 4:16-18)**

We are told to watch and pray that we might **escape** the tribulation period. **(Luke 21:36)**

We should study the Bible and understand the symbolism of the festivals, so that we won't be easily deceived regarding doctrine concerning the end times. **(2 Thessalonians 2:1-2)**

We should love the nation of Israel and the Jewish people. We should provoke the Jews to jealousy by understanding and celebrating the festivals. **(Romans 11:13-14)**

We should read the book of Revelation as there is a blessing for those who do. **(Revelation 1:3)**

We will be happy and walk in favor if we understand the blessings symbolized by the feasts!

Blessed (happy, fortunate, to be envied) are the people who know the joyful sound [who understand and appreciate the spiritual blessings symbolized by the feasts]; they walk, O Lord, in the light and favor of Your countenance! In Your name they rejoice all the day, and in Your righteousness they are exalted. (Psalms 89:15-16 Amplified)

GLOSSARY

1. **Yeshua** is the Hebraic name for Jesus. It means "salvation."
2. **Rosh-Hodesh** is the name for the first day of every month in the Hebrew calendar marked by the appearance of the new moon. The new moon in the Hebrew calendar is marked by the day and hour that the new crescent is observed. It is considered a minor holiday.
3. **Shabbat** is the Jewish day of rest and the seventh day of the week. Shabbat observance entails refraining from work and engaging in restful activities to honor the day. It is usually observed from sunset Friday evening until sunset Saturday night.
4. **Mikveh** is a bath used for the purpose of ritual immersion in Judaism. Several biblical regulations specify that full immersion in water is required to regain ritual purity after ritually impure incidents have occurred (such as touching a dead body). It is also applied to some changes of status in life (such as marriage). In undergoing

the mikveh waters, one is said to be "reborn" or "born again."

5. **Torah** can mean the first five books of the Bible (Genesis, Exodus, Leviticus, Numbers and Deuteronomy), or it can sometimes be used to mean the totality of Jewish teaching and practice. God gave the Torah to Moses.

6. **Oral Law** was transmitted by God to Moses and from him handed down to other religious leaders of each generation. The oral instruction was ultimately recorded in the Talmud and the Mishnah.

7. **Mishnah** is the written account of the Oral Law. It consists of six orders each containing 7–12 tractates, 63 in total, and further subdivided into chapters and paragraphs or verses. The subjects are: *Zeraim* (Seeds), dealing with prayer and blessings, tithes and agricultural laws; *Moed* (Festival), pertaining to the laws of the Sabbath and the Festivals; *Nashim* (Women), concerning marriage and divorce, some forms of oaths and the laws of the Nazarite; *Nezikin* (Damages), dealing with civil and criminal law, the functioning of the courts and oaths; *Kodashim* (Holy things), regarding sacrificial rites, the Temple, and the dietary laws; and *Tehorot* (Purities), pertaining to the laws of purity and impurity, including the impurity of the dead, the laws of food purity and bodily purity.

8. The **Talmud**, has two components. The first part is the Mishnah, which is Judaism's Oral Law in written form. The second part is the Gemara that is the commentary on the Oral Law and other

subjects. The terms Talmud and Gemara are often used interchangeably. The whole Talmud consists of 63 tractates, and is over 6,200 pages long. The Talmud contains the teachings and opinions of thousands of rabbis on a variety of subjects. The Talmud is the basis for all codes of Jewish law and is much quoted in rabbinic literature.

9.   **Orthodox Judaism** is the approach to religious Judaism that adheres to the interpretation and application of the laws and ethics of the Torah as legislated in the Talmudic texts by the Sanhedrin. Orthodox Judaism was mainstream until around 200 years ago when the Reform movement began in Germany. Since then, a number of non-Orthodox movements within Judaism have developed.

10. **Ethics of the Fathers** is a compilation of the ethical teachings of the Rabbis of the Mishnaic period (200 CE).

11. The **Babylonian exile** (or **Babylonian captivity**) is the name generally given to the deportation and exile of the Jews of the ancient Kingdom of Judah to Babylon by Nebuchadnezzar II. The exile in Babylon occurred in three waves from 597 to 581 BCE. The destruction of the Temple occurred during this time. After Cyrus the Great of Persia conquered Babylon, he allowed the exiles to return in 537 BCE.

12. The **Tribulation Period** refers to a future seven-year period of time when God is judging the unbelieving world and dealing with the nation of

Israel. It is known as **Jacob's Trouble (Jeremiah 30:7)**. It is also known as the **birth pains** and is referenced in **Matthew 24.** It is also referred to as **the time of indignation** in the book of Daniel. The Apostle John describes the tumultuous events that will take place during this time period in the Book of Revelation.

13. **Hanukkah,** also known as the **Festival of Lights** and **Feast of Dedication**, is an eight-day Jewish holiday commemorating the rededication of the Temple in Jerusalem at the time of the Maccabean Revolt against the Greeks in the 2nd century BCE. Hanukkah is observed for eight nights and days, starting on the 25th day of Kislev according to the Hebrew calendar, which may occur at any time from late November to late December on the Gregorian calendar.

14. The **Apocrypha** denotes the collection of ancient books found in some editions of the Bible. Catholic and Orthodox Christians regard them as fully canonical, although most Protestants do not.

15. The **Epistle of Barnabas** dates from the late 1st or early 2nd century and is traditionally ascribed to Barnabas who is mentioned in the Acts of the Apostles. (It is not to be confused with the Gospel of Barnabas.)

16. The **Haggadah** is the book containing the story of the Exodus and the ritual order of the Seder meal celebrated at Passover. It is a fulfillment of the Scriptural commandment to each Jew to "tell your son" of the Jewish liberation from slavery in Egypt as described in the book of Exodus: *"**And**

thou shalt tell thy son in that day, saying: It is because of that which the LORD did for me when I came forth out of Egypt." (Exodus 13:8)

17. The **Gemara** is the component of the Talmud that includes rabbinical analysis and commentary on the Mishnah. After the Mishnah was published in 200 CE, the work was studied exhaustively by generation after generation of rabbis in Babylon and Israel. Their discussions were written down in a series of books that became the Gemara, which when combined with the Mishnah constituted the Talmud.

18. **Book of Jubilees** is an apocryphal book of the Old Testament that retells the book of Genesis and part of Exodus. It is believed that Enoch may have written it.

19. **Midrash** is a form of rabbinic literature. There are two types of midrash: midrash aggada and midrash halakha. Midrash aggada can best be described as a form of storytelling that explores ethics and values in biblical texts. Midrash halakha focuses on Jewish law and practice.

20. **Reform Judaism** maintains that Judaism and Jewish traditions should be modernized and made compatible with the surrounding culture.

21. **Genesis Rabba** is a religious text comprising a collection of ancient rabbinical interpretations of the Book of Genesis.

22. The **Babylonian Talmud** was written about 200 years after the Jerusalem Talmud. It is often seen as more authoritative and is studied more than the Jerusalem Talmud. In general, the terms

Gemara or *Talmud* without further qualification refer to the "Babylonian Talmud."

23. **Moses Maimonides** was a preeminent Spanish, Sephardic Jewish rabbi, philosopher, astronomer, and one of the most prolific and influential Torah scholars and physicians of the Middle Ages. His fourteen-volume Mishnah Torah still carries significant authority as a codification of Talmudic law.

24. **Hephzibah** was a symbolic name, used by Isaiah the prophet, along with Beulah, to describe the salvation of Zion.

25. **Beulah** was a symbolic name, along with Hephzibah, used by Isaiah the prophet to describe the salvation of Zion.

26. **Mussaf Service** is the additional prayer service recited for the Sabbath and festivals. It takes the place of additional offerings that were once made on these days.

27. **Mercy Seat** was the cover that rested upon the Ark of the Covenant. The Ark of the Covenant is a chest that contained the Tablets of Stone that the Ten Commandments were inscribed upon.

28. **Book of Enoch** is an ancient book, traditionally ascribed to Enoch, the great-grandfather of Noah. It is not in the Biblical canon, but Jude refers to it the New Testament. **(Jude 1:14-15)**

Selected Bibliography

Agnon, S.Y. **Days of Awe**. New York: Schocken Books, 1965, 1975, 1995.

Chumney, Edward. **The Seven Festivals of the Messiah**. Pennsylvania: Destiny Image, 1994.

Conner, Kevin J. **The Feasts of Israel**. Oregon: Bible Temple, 1980.

Eckstein, Rabbi Yechiel. **What You Should Know About Jews and Judaism.** Texas: Word Books, 1984.

Edersheim, Alfred. **The Temple: Its Ministry and Services**. Grand Rapids: Eerdmans, 1972.

Gaster, Theodor H. **Festivals of the Jewish Year.** New York: Morrow Quill Paperbacks, 1978.

Glaser, Mitch and Zhava. **The Fall Feasts of Israel**. Chicago: Moody Bible Institute, 1987.

Good, Joseph. **Rosh HaShanah and the Messianic Kingdom to Come**. Texas: Hatikva Ministries, 1989, 1998.

Heidler, Robert D. **The Cycles of God.** Texas: Glory of Zion Ministries, 2006.

Helyer, Larry R., PhD, and Wagner, Richard. **The Book of Revelation for Dummies.** New Jersey: Wiley Publishing, Inc., 2008.

Stone, Perry. **40 Days of Teshuvah**. Tennessee: Voice of Evangelism, 2006.

Zimmerman, Martha. **Celebrate the Feasts.** Minneapolis: Bethany House, 1981.

Appendix I

BIRTH OF YESHUA AT SUKKOT

It can be calculated mathematically that Yeshua was born during the season of *Sukkot* (Feast of Tabernacles).

To calculate the date, three things must be established:

1. The date that the angel Gabriel tells Zachariah (father of John the Baptist) about his son's birth. The birthdate of John is established by going forward nine months.
2. The approximate date of Mary's conception of Yeshua.
3. The date of Herod's death.

We read in **Luke 1:5**, that Zachariah is a priest of the division of Abijah. Israel was divided into 24 districts at the time of Yeshua. Each of these districts sent two representatives to officiate at the Temple during the weeks of the year. In **1 Chronicles 24**, the first division of priests would serve in the first week of the year, which would be both in the month of Aviv and the month of Tishri since both months begin the new year. (Aviv is the first month on the religious calendar and Tishri is the first month on the civil calendar.)

During the third week in the month of Aviv, the priests from all 24 districts would come to the Temple to help during the week of Passover. This would also be the case for the festival of *Shavuot* (Pentecost) and for the festival of *Sukkot* (Feast of Tabernacles) when all males were required to go to Jerusalem as specified by God in **Deuteronomy 16:16.**

In **1 Chronicles 24:10**, we see that Abijah was the eighth division or course of priests. The first course served in the first week of the year (Aviv); the second course, the second week; etc. The course of Abijah would minister during the tenth week of the first half of the year. Remember, the weeks of *Pesach* (Passover) and *Shavuot* (Pentecost) would not be counted because all the priests were required to go to Jerusalem then.

In **Luke 1:9-10**, we see that Zachariah is burning incense. This is done in the room of the Temple known as the Holy Place. As incense is being burned in the Temple, 18 special prayers are prayed. These 18 prayers would be prayed every day in the Temple. One of these prayers is that Elijah would come. This is important because it was understood by the people that Elijah would precede the coming of the Messiah as stated in **Malachi 4:5.**

These 18 special prayers would be prayed twice a day, once in the morning and once in the afternoon. In **Luke 1:11-13**, Gabriel appeared and told Zachariah that his prayer was heard and John the Baptist would be born. John the Baptist was not literally Elijah, but was of the spirit and power of Elijah. **(Luke 1:17)**

Allowing two weeks for the laws of separation that God commanded in **Leviticus 12:5; 15:19,24-25** after going back to the house **(Luke 1:23)** and then going forward nine months (Sivan [tenth week] + 2 weeks + 9 months) puts the birth of John the Baptist during the festival of *Pesach* (Passover). This is an extremely important point because during the Passover Seder, the people are instructed by God to go to the door during one part of the service and look for Elijah while the Seder meal is eaten. There is a cup on the table that is called **the cup of Elijah.** Yeshua said that John the Baptist was the "Elijah to come."

In **Luke 1:26** during the sixth month of Elisabeth's pregnancy, the angel Gabriel appeared to Mary, the cousin of Elizabeth. This should have been around the twenty-fifth of Kislev, otherwise known as Hanukkah. During the time of the first century, Hanukkah was known as the second Sukkot (Feast of Tabernacles). During the time of Hanukkah, all of the Sukkot prayers are prayed once again. Mary's dialogue with the angel Gabriel is found in the liturgy of Sukkot (Feast of Tabernacles) today. If you calculate from the twenty-fifth of Kislev and add eight days for the festival of Hanukkah plus nine months for Mary's pregnancy, this will bring you to the time of the festival of Sukkot, or Tishri 15. On Tishri 22, known as *Shemini Atzeret,* or the "eighth day," Yeshua was circumcised. **(Luke 2:22-23)**

How do we know that Zechariah was given the prophecy about John in the first half of the year rather than the last? The key is found in the life and death of

King Herod. In **Matthew 2**, Herod is visited by "wise men from the East." The "wise men" were probably Jewish rabbis as they were known as *chakamim,* which means "wise men." The "land of the East" was the land of *Babylon.* **(Genesis 29:1, Judges 6:3).** During this time, the largest Jewish population was in Babylon. Even though Ezra, Nehemiah, and others had returned, most of the people had remained behind.

There was a prophecy in **Numbers 24:17**, that a star would be related to the coming of the Messiah. Knowing this prophecy, the wise men would have traveled to Jerusalem to do homage.

It has been taught that the wise men appeared about a year to 18 months after the birth of Yeshua. This was based upon Herod's killing of the male children less than two years, according to the date that the wise men had given him for the appearance of the star. **(Matthew 2:7-8, 16)**

It was the custom in ancient Israel to count the years of one's age from the date of conception. Therefore, Herod killed the children one year old and under according to the way that age is calculated today. The wise men must have arrived in Jerusalem just prior or at the time of Yeshua's birth.

The fact that He was born in a stable is a clue to the time of His birth! In Hebrew, a "stable" is called a *sukkah.* **(Genesis 33:17)** Sukkot, the name of this festival, is the plural of the word sukkah.

Joseph and Mary bring Yeshua into Jerusalem 40 days after His birth for His dedication in the Temple. Prior to that time, God had warned Joseph in a dream to flee to Egypt. This indicates that Herod must have died during that period of time. As long as Herod was alive, they could not appear at the Temple.

If we could determine the approximate date of Herod's death, it would establish the season of Yeshua's birth. The Jewish historian, Josephus, who lived during the first century CE, documents the details of Herod's death. According to Josephus, he died around September in the fourth year before the Common Era.

With the knowledge that Herod died in the Fall, the same time of year as the festival of Sukkot, and that his death was within 40 days of the birth of Yeshua, it can be established that Messiah was born at this time of year.

CPSIA information can be obtained at www.ICGtesting.com
Printed in the USA
LVOW01s1150120114

369093LV00009B/46/P